God's Heart for Women

JOLANDE BIJL

GOD'S HEART FOR WOMEN

God's Heart for Women
Jolande Bijl

Cover design and inside: Jonathan Reining, Jore Ontwerp
English Translation: Hope Visser, Elkanah Translations
Editing: Helen Birkbeck Language & Editorial Services
Originally published in Dutch in 2020: "Gods hart voor vrouwen".
Steventure, The Netherlands

Illustrations on page 14, 17, 70, 72: Stations of the Cross and on page 87:
Madonna and child are embroidered by Frédérique Moussault.
The other images in this book fall under the public domain copyright.
If we have overlooked something, please contact us.

ISBN 978-90-83043-0-1-2
NUR 707

For all Bible references, the New International Version (NIV) has been
used unless otherwise indicated.

TABLE OF CONTENTS

"What if Paul did not actually
mean that women should
always remain silent?"

PREFACE

Last year my friend Steven read the book *Why Not Women?* by Loren Cunningham and David J. Hamilton, an extensive, in-depth Bible study on the subject of women in ministry. Precisely because it was such an in-depth study, it took some effort to get through it, but the message is truly awesome, and we soon found ourselves thinking that more people should hear this message! Initially we wanted to take the core message of Why Not Women? and put it into simple wording so that it would be easily accessible for a larger group of people, but, once we started, our enthusiasm increased because we kept discovering new things in the Bible. Steven provided the input and I wrote it down. This is how *God's Heart for Women* came to be.

The core message of *Why Not Women?* revolves around the question: what about women in the church: should they remain silent or not? In some churches women are not allowed to lead or even to speak, but in other churches they are. So what about that verse in which Paul says that women should remain silent? "Women should remain silent in the churches. They are not allowed to speak, but must be in submission, as the law says" (1 Corinthians 14:34). We cannot just ignore those words, can we?

But what if Paul did not actually mean that women should always remain silent and we have misunderstood this verse – that would mean that all this time we have not allowed women to live out their calling. Women whom God may have called to speak and lead, but who were not given the chance because we did not understand the Bible verse on this.

In this book we will take a look at the "problematic verses" on the role of women in the church. We will do this by searching the Bible for God's heart for women. What was God's intention for women and men? How did Jesus, and later Paul, treat women? We will also take a look at the culture in which Jesus was born so that we can place the verses in context. Then it is up to you to answer the question of whether or not women should be allowed to speak and lead in the church, for yourself.

We hope that through this book you will draw closer to God's heart and that you will be blessed by its message, which is truly valuable for both women and men!

Steven and Jolande

"Women in the Bible show
how God can work through
women in a beautiful way."

INTRODUCTION

Here in the West, women are not doing badly at all. There are plenty of examples of women who successfully lead businesses. Just take a look at thenextwomen. com, an initiative of several successful female entrepreneurs. Their slogan is: "You cannot become what you cannot see." The reason why we have more strong male leaders is that female leaders are less visible, according to TheNextWomen. That is why their goal is to shine a spotlight on successful female role models. It is easier to follow a good example if you can see it.

For Christian women there are role models that let us see and experience how beautifully God can work through women. Who has not heard of Joyce Meyer, Beth Moore or Corrie ten Boom? Granted, modern Dutch female speakers are not on the tip of my tongue; I would really have to sit down and think about it. The men are in the majority in the pulpit.

And yet we women have also been given role models by God. We too can become what we see women do in the Bible. It helps me to look at the strong women in the Bible, especially in moments when I feel inadequate as a woman. They encourage and strengthen me to do what God has called me to do – even if it goes against the tide sometimes.

Just take a look at Sheerah,[1] for example. You have probably never heard of her, but she built three cities that are still around today: Lower and Upper Beth Horon and Uzzen Sheerah.[2] The first two were no ordinary cities; they were built in strategic locations. They played an important part in the defense and protection of Israel, as history later showed. Joshua defeated the Amorites there, for example.[3] Uzzen Sheerah means "ear of Sheerah", or, in other words," listen to Sheerah". She was a strategic builder and her voice was heard.

Or take a look at Claudia, another woman who has remained invisible to many. Her name is not mentioned in the Bible; we call her the wife of Pilate. Sources other than the Bible give her the name Claudia Procula.

She was the granddaughter of the Roman emperor Augustus, so she was a princess. She must have been a courageous woman. Jesus was going to be executed as an innocent man. People of that time could have known this, because Isaiah had prophesied that Jesus would not do anything wrong but would be led to the slaughter like an innocent lamb.[4] Just before Jesus was crucified, God wanted to highlight this truth about Jesus once more, and He did it through a dream. A dream He gave to a woman, Claudia. Jesus was brought before Pilate, her husband, who as the governor and judge would have to decide His fate. The chief priests and leaders had accused Jesus of all kinds of injustices, but Pilate was surprised that Jesus did not answer them. In order to cool the heated exchange with the leaders, Pilate offered them Barabbas. Let them crucify him and release Jesus, because once a year a prisoner was allowed to be released. The leaders were not satisfied with this at all; Jesus had to be crucified. Pilate was under great pressure, because they needed his permission to crucify Jesus. At that moment a message from Claudia was brought into the court.[5] Did she go to him herself or did he receive a written message? We don't know. Claudia had had a dream the night before and she was not afraid to disturb her husband while he was working. This is

Pilate gets a message from his wife: "Stay out of this. Last night I had a dream about this man."

quite remarkable when you know that women in those days had no voice in legal matters and a court did not even consider them to be reliable witnesses. But this woman knew that Jesus was righteous, because God had showed her that in a dream. She had witnessed what was to happen to Jesus. "Don't have anything to do with that innocent man, for I have suffered a great deal today in a dream because of him," is what she told him, and she advised her husband: "Don't dirty your hands with Him. Stay out of this".[6] When Pilate saw that he was not getting anywhere, he washed his hands in front of the crowd and said: "I am innocent of this man's blood. It is your responsibility!"[7]

The Eastern Orthodox Church gave Claudia a place of honor by declaring her a saint.[8] She was a woman who was admired for her courage.

There are a few more women who inspire me: Shiphrah and Puah. "Shiphrah" means beauty, charm and "Puah" means gleaming. Two beautiful, beaming women. They were midwives in Egypt and helped the Hebrew women when they were giving birth. The Pharaoh had said: "When you help the Hebrew women give birth, check to see if it is a boy or a girl. You must kill the boys." But the two women honored God and had respect for the sanctity of life, so they allowed the boys to live. Pharaoh had the women brought before him and asked them why they allowed the boys to live. They told him that the Hebrew women were stronger than the Egyptian women. "By the time we get there, the child is already born." They obviously would not be intimidated by the Pharaoh. God rewarded these two women with families of their own and the Hebrew people multiplied and grew strong.[9] One of the boys who was not killed, in spite of Pharaoh's orders, was Moses.

These were two powerful women! They dared to defy the will of the Pharaoh and were not afraid to face him when he called them in for questioning. With incredible bravery they stood their ground as they showed him that there is something bigger than the will of man, even if that man is the king himself. God is greater, and they remained faithful to their calling to fight for new life.

There is another woman who is not named in the Bible. She is mentioned first as being in the courtyard of the high priest, where a group of people are warming themselves by a fire. Peter is also there. Suddenly a woman's voice is heard – the voice of the servant girl, according to the Bible – claiming: "You were with the Nazarene!"

Suddenly there was a woman's voice: "You were part of that group!" Peter panicked and said: "Oh, go away. I don't even know him." Somewhere far away a rooster crowed, because it was morning.

Thus she confronts Peter, who has been waiting anonymously among the group of people to see what would happen to Jesus. Panicked, Peter denies, in front of all those people, that he has been with Jesus. "I do not know the man," he declares. "Yes," the girl says to those standing there, "he was one of them. I recognize him."[10] Here yet again is a woman who is not afraid to speak the truth, even though it was uncommon in those days for a woman to speak to a man like that. Especially a servant girl.

These are just a few examples of powerful women in the Bible. And I haven't even mentioned the more well-known examples, such as Esther, who dared to speak to King Xerxes and by doing so saved her entire people. When you go through the Bible, you will find many more powerful women. So when did this whole discussion start about the position of women in the church, a discussion that turned out to be to the disadvantage of women? Somewhere during the course of history Christian women were sidelined and it was decided that the men were to arrange things. Are we brave enough to take a look once again at those verses that say women are not allowed to speak, in the context in which they were written? In order to do that we will need to explore the cultures that influenced the world in which Jesus was born – the cultures of the Greeks, the Romans and the Jewish rabbis. Otherwise, we cannot understand what the verses meant in the context of their time.

This will be an exciting journey, because you will discover that these cultures were shockingly hostile to women. Our intention, however, is not to deride cultures, but to discover God's heart for women, straight through all cultures and experiences. God's heart for people – men and women – can be seen when you look at Jesus, for He is the perfect image of God. How did Jesus treat women? We are going to look at that in depth. Here is a small preview:

Did you know that, at the most important moments in Jesus' earthly life, it was mostly women who were in the spotlight? That is how valuable women were to Him!

- At his birth Mary played an important role, of course. Jesus was born of God and from the seed of the woman.[11] That went totally against the common view. In ancient times people believed that children came from the seed of the man and that women were no more than the fertile soil in which the baby could grow.

- When Jesus performed His first miracle, Mary, his mother, again played an important role. They were at a wedding and the wine ran out. Mary spoke to Jesus about this. Even though Jesus told her He was not going to do anything about it, because His "time had not yet come", Mary told the servants: "Whatever He tells you to do, do it!" The servants listened to her. It was partially owing to her speaking up that Jesus performed His first miracle at the wedding.[12]

- Just before his death, Jesus was anointed by a woman.[13] Anointing was a common ritual in Bible times. Kings, priests and prophets were anointed when they were installed, like Aaron for example, when he was anointed as priest[14] and David when he became king.[15] Anointing was a ritual performed by men, but Jesus allowed Himself to be anointed by a woman and said that everyone would hear about what she had done.

- After rising from the dead Jesus first appeared to a woman, Mary Magdalene. She and the other Mary were the first people to be commanded by Jesus to spread the gospel that He had risen from the grave.[16] Once again, women were in the spotlight on this momentous occasion in Jesus' life.

Mary Magdalene (painted by Jan van Scorel, ca 1530) is traditionally depicted with a vessel of ointment, in reference to the Anointing of Jesus. The Bible however, does not mention that it was Mary Magdalene who anointed Jesus.

And Paul: how did he view women? I sometimes hear people say that they struggle with Paul because of his encouraging women to cover their heads and be silent in church. They assume therefore that Paul must not have been an advocate for women in ministry. Yet his admiration for women – including those who worked alongside him as leaders – cannot be denied, as we will see later on.

In the life of Paul, we can also see women playing a major role on special occasions. One of those women is Lydia. We read in the Bible that she was an entre-preneur, a seller of purple dye or cloth from the city of Thyatira, who served God but had never heard the gospel of Jesus. Then she met Paul and his friends and listened to the good news that they had come to bring. As she listened, God opened her heart. The message really touched her; she wanted to be part of this! She was saved and she and her entire household were baptized.[17]

And do you know what makes this so amazing? Lydia was the first European Christian. And… she was a woman! How special that must have been in her culture, where men led the way. But God thinks differently. Join us as we seek God's heart for women and be amazed by His goodness!

"According to Aristotle,
women are actually
failed men."

CHAPTER 1

WOMEN IN THE ANCIENT GREEK CULTURE

The way Jesus treated women was radical for His time. How truly radical it was does not become clear until we understand the cultural context of His words and actions. That is why we will first take a look at history. We will explore the ancient Greek culture, at the time of Homer, Socrates and Plato, because this culture greatly influenced how people thought at the time when Jesus was growing up, and still greatly influences our Western mindset. How did the ancient Greeks view women? Of course, we cannot generalize everything, but we will get a pretty good impression of the ancient Greek line of thought when we look at Greek poets and sages of that time.

In the *Iliad,* a story by the poet Homer set around the year 1240 BC, we can read how women were claimed by men as spoils of war, to then be made their slaves or mistresses. We also read how women were supposed to be the cause of conflict and were responsible for all the suffering in the world.[18]

From the mythology we also get a general idea of how women were viewed. The Greek god Zeus was married to his sister, Hera. She was considered the goddess of marriage and the symbol of fertility, but in many mythological stories she is portrayed as a jealous wife. Her husband is not faithful to her and has countless offspring with other goddesses. With such an example it is no wonder that adultery was common among the men of those times.[19]

Besides Homer, another ancient Greek poet by the name of Hesiod wrote in his poem *Theogony* that there was once a time when men lived a life of bliss without the presence of women. This paradise is lost when Prometheus steals fire from the gods of Olympus and shares it with other men. As a result, Zeus decides to place a curse on the world that will fill men's hearts with joy when they embrace it: he has Hephaestus, the craftsman

Top:
Homer,
Hesiod (r)

Middle:
Plato,
Aristotle (r)

Bottom:
Demosthenes,
Solon (r)

among the gods, form a woman and calls her Pandora. A wonderful creation, irresistible to men, she is, however, given a mean character. "From her comes the female race, the deadly race that lives among mortal men to their great misery," he says.[20]

Pandora is gifted to Epimetheus, the dumber brother of Prometheus, who takes her as his wife. Epimetheus has a box filled with special contents in his home and when Pandora, who cannot control her curiosity, removes the lid of this box, all kinds of misery and countless disasters fly out of it immediately and spread all over the world. Only hope is left in the box, because Pandora managed to replace the lid just in time. But the damage had been done and since then humanity has been tormented by all kinds of illnesses and famines.[21] Here too we can read how the woman is deemed the source of all kinds of evil.

The Greek poet Simonides, who lived during a later period, wrote that men and women do not share a common source, as if women did not belong to the same human race. He was known for his aversion to women, which can be seen in all kinds of satirical expressions in which he compares every type of woman to an animal. He called women angry foxes or stubborn donkeys.[22]

It was in this Greek culture, full of negative references to women, that the philosophical celebrities Socrates, Plato and later Aristotle lived. The latter was to become the teacher of Alexander the Great. Through his conquests, Greek thinking spread throughout the entire Mediterranean area, part of which was the civilization in which Jesus was born.

There were also prominent men in Athens who did acknowledge the value of women. Aristophanes included women with strong personalities in his plays and also referred to the stupidity of men. Socrates recognized several women because of their insight.

According to Plato, however, women are so obstinate that they will never listen. Women should just get undressed and become the common property of men who want sex. Bad men, according to Plato, would be reincarnated as women; that was how women came to be.

Of the men who were (...) cowards or who had led an unjust life, we can reasonably assume that they have changed into women in the next generation.
Plato (in Timaeus)

He suggests that a few women be selected and trained to have sex with the leaders of the state. It should be noted that Plato did think that women should be educated.

Plato's student Aristotle provided biological arguments for his theory of why a woman was of less value than a man. A woman was actually a *failed* man. During conception something went wrong, causing a female fetus to be formed with a few physical defects into the bargain. A woman is therefore a deviation from the norm: the man. Because she cannot produce seed, she is therefore an infertile man. The Greek philosophers and scientists believed that seed carried life, because it was said to contain miniature beings. Men were therefore the unilateral source of life, while women were only the fertile soil in which this life could grow. Aristotle advised men to keep themselves separate from women, as that was more divine.[23]

> *The relationship of man to woman is that of a natural supe-rior to a natural subordinate, that of a ruler to a ruled.*
> **Aristotle (in Politics)**

Solon of Athens was the first famous political leader of his city. In order to promote prostitution, he created laws allowing for women to become possessions that could be purchased and sold. He purchased slave girls whom he then placed naked on the streets so that they could become common property and be available to whomever paid for them. The income went to the government.

Later on, political leaders said that women should be locked indoors, where they should live in solitary confinement. Women had no rights and no access to education. They were ruled by their father, then by their husband and later by their sons.

A contemporary of Demosthenes, who was considered the best orator in Athens, said in a speech: "After all, we have mistresses for pleasure, concubines for daily body maintenance, but wives to make legitimate children and to be a reliable keeper of the household to have."[24]

Women were of little value. Their only destiny was to produce and raise children. We see a poignant example of this in a letter from a polder boy, Hilarion, to his wife, who has stayed behind in their village of Oxyrhynchus, while he is still doing a job with part of the team to which he belongs. Written in the year 1 BC:

Hilarion salutes his sister Alis and my Mother Berus and Apollinaris.

Know that we are still in Alexandria today; don't be afraid when the others (of my team) come home; I stay in Alexandria; I ask you and remind you to take care of the child; as soon as I get paid wages, I will send you something. When you give birth with God's help - if it's a boy, save it, if it's a girl, then abandon it.

Girls were allowed to be abandoned anywhere, even if alive and well, and just thrown out with the trash. There was no law prohibiting this. They were too expensive and would not be able to care for their parents in their old age.

Much of what we know about women in ancient Greece we know because of what upper-class Greek men in Athens wrote down. That is how we know that upper-class women were limited in their social life. They received little education and were not allowed to say much. They were allowed to leave the house only if accompanied by a man, and, even then, they had to cover their face. Upper-class men had a lot more freedom than the women. When girls entered puberty, they often had to marry men who were three times their age. Once married, they had to do the household chores.

In ancient Sparta at that time, the situation for women was much better. In his *Odyssey* Homer calls the area surrounding Sparta *Sparte kalligynaika*, in other words "the Sparta of beautiful women". Wealthy men from Athens viewed the women of Sparta as strange and self-assured, very different from the women in Athens. In Sparta the men were trained from a young age to be soldiers and lived mostly in barracks. Because the men were absent, the women of Sparta had a lot of responsibilities. They took part in sports, learned how to hunt, read and write and were encouraged to be assertive. Men and women were treated more like equals there and the women married men of their own age. The women were even encouraged to sleep with lovers in order to have more children, because there were always too few of those.

CHAPTER 2

WOMEN IN THE ROMAN EMPIRE

The power of the Greeks eventually diminished and the Romans began to become dominant, but the influence of the highly developed Greek culture remained. The first great Roman poet, Virgil, started to write myths based on the life of the Greek Homer. Virgil gives the Romans gods and goddesses like those of the Greeks, with the same negative views on women.

According to Virgil, the Romans were the descendants of Aeneas from defeated Troy. During his flight from Troy to Italy, he is attacked by the goddess of marriage, Juno (in Greek mythology Hera), but the goddess Venus (in Greek mythology Aphrodite) comes to his rescue. Venus is the seductive goddess of erotic love, adultery and prostitution. She is also the mother of Aeneas; however, they still go to bed with each other.

Thanks to Virgil the Romans now also had a divine origin, just like the Greeks. Venus set the tone for how the Roman empire viewed women.

The hatred of women had by then increased so much that the Roman emperor Augustus had to persuade men to marry at all. Marriage had been reduced to a compulsory act, something that was necessary in order to reproduce. The Roman author Aulus Gellius wrote the following in his *Noctes Atticae*:

If we could do without a woman, citizens of Rome, we would all avoid that annoyance, but because nature has determined that we can neither live comfortably with them nor completely without them, we must ensure our survival, in instead of choosing our temporary convenience.[25]

The influential Roman poet Ovid encouraged men to cheat and to have multiple mistresses. Women were tricksters and could never be trusted, because they were the daughters of the unreliable goddess Venus.

Because women were regarded as inferior, they often did not receive a name of their own. They were given their father's surname. Their sisters often got the same name.

Venus, Roman goddess of love

In addition to Aeneas, the illegitimate son of the goddess Venus, the Romans also descended from Aeneas' descendant Romulus, the founder of the city of Rome. Romulus was the son of Mars, the god of war. They named the closest planets Mars and Venus. According to the Romans, the ideal man was a warrior, like Mars, and the ideal woman a sexual partner, like Venus. Under Roman law, a man was allowed to kill his wife for adultery or drunkenness without consequences. On the other hand, a man was allowed to commit adultery without consequences.

Just as with the Greeks, the Romans would place unwanted children outside to die. Usually this was done to girls. Romulus later set up laws to protect boys and first-born girls from this practice. Otherwise too many baby girls would be killed and there would be too few women to provide successors. In both the Greek and Roman empires there were many more men than women.

As the Roman empire developed and grew, views on women progressed. While the Greeks remained narrow-minded when it came to women (the level at which this occurred differed by area and period), the Romans slowly progressed. Women received an education, if they were from wealthy families. But because the Romans had built their nation on a military system and many of the leaders were from the army, this automatically ensured that women could never take the same position as men in that system.

We will conclude with a few facts on Roman women in the time of Jesus[26]:

- In the 19th century a sarcophagus was discovered that belonged to a young lady named Crepereia Tryphaena, who probably lived in the second century in Rome. She probably died just before she was to be married. The custom was that young women would then turn in their toys. Crepereia was buried with her ivory doll and a box of doll's clothes. Her doll did not have a Barbie-like figure, but wide hips and a big belly. The message that had been hammered home to this young woman was that she was destined to be a mother – the most appreciated achievement for a Roman woman.

- The upbringing of women was a controversial subject in the Roman period. Most girls in middle- and upper-class families learned the basic skills of reading and writing, while some families took it a step further and hired private tutors to teach their daughters grammar and Greek. This was all meant to prepare a girl for her future role as caretaker of the home and to make her a more interesting companion for her husband. Many Romans believed, however, that women would become irritating nags if they received too much education. In fact, they thought intellectual independence would lead to sexual escapades. Yet some of the elite families encouraged their daughters to become highly educated. The most famous example of this was probably Hortensia, the daughter of Cicero's greatest courtroom rival, Quintus Hortensius Hortalus. She is one of the few Roman women who was famous as an orator. In 42 BC, Hortensia eloquently (and with some success) denounced in the Roman forum a new tax that the richest women of Rome were to pay to help finance the war.

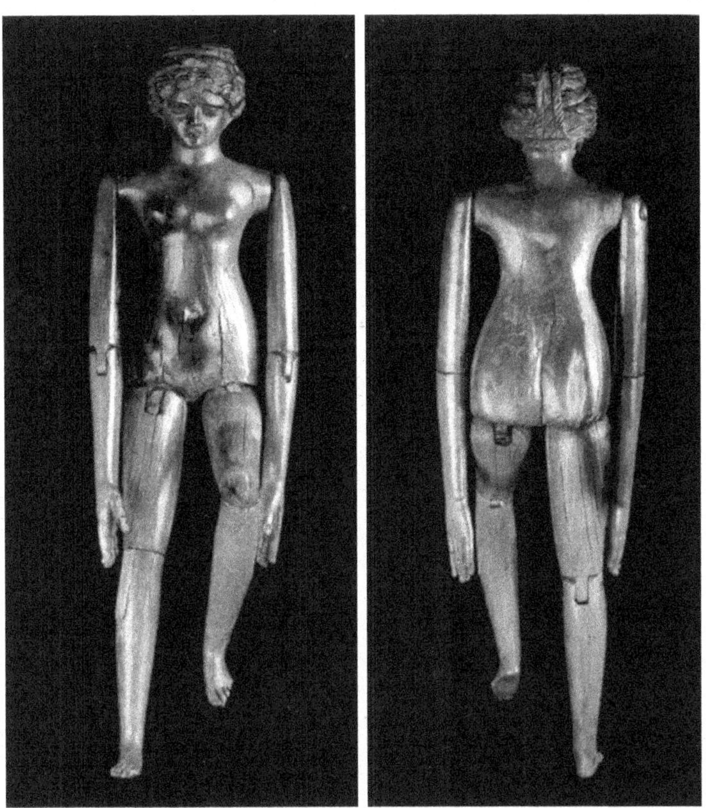

Roman version of the Barbie doll with the ideal figure of a mother: wide hips and round belly.

CHAPTER 3

WOMEN IN THE JEWISH CULTURE

In the Old Testament we find beautiful examples of women who were greatly respected.

Deborah was a prophetess who led Israel as a judge. She lived under the palm tree of Deborah and the Israelites went to her to obtain her judgment on important matters.[27]

Huldah was a prophetess who lived in Jerusalem during the reign of King Josiah. Prominent men, the priest for example, would go to speak with her.[28]

David praised his future wife Abigail for her wise insight and advice that prevented him from making a huge mistake.[29]

Deborah, prophetess and judge of Israel. Her intervention brought peace to the land for 40 years.

A wise woman is a gift from God, according to Solomon, and he was one of the wisest men who ever lived or will live.[30]

After a period of time the Jewish culture changed and the situation for Jewish women deteriorated. Jewish rabbis started to add their own writings, the Mishna and the Talmud, to the Bible. Jesus referred to these sometimes, when He accused the teachers of the law of His time that they were laying heavy burdens on the people and making God's commands powerless because of their own traditions.[31]

This Jewish literature (which you can read here: https://www.sefaria.org/texts) was originally written by men, for men. It does speak of women, but where are the female authors? Their absence is striking, and they would remain absent until about the 19th century, with a few exceptions here and there. Women seemed to have no place in the Jewish religion, so they were not taught. Here is a selection from the traditions, from which you can see how men thought about women:

The one who teaches his daughter the Torah is considered as having taught her foolishness.[32]

A man should not instruct his daughter in the Torah because most women do not intend to be instructed in it, but on the contrary are inclined to deduce matters from the Torah. Nonsense, of course, in relation to the inferiority of their mind.[33]

The snake seduced Eve into having sexual relationships with him. When the snake came upon Eve, he infected her with moral contamination, and this contagion remained in all people.[34]

Whatever a man wants to do with his wife, he can do it. He can enter into sexual contact with her in any desired way, because she is just like the butcher's meat: if he wants to eat it with salt, he can eat it that way. If he wants to eat it roasted, he may eat it roasted.[35]

Women and children are not allowed to read the Torah in public, because that would not be respectful of the community.[36]

One hundred women are worth as much as two men.[37]

What were Jewish women not allowed to do, for example (that men were)?

In practice, Jewish women were at a disadvantage on a number of points compared to men at that time. Jewish women were restricted in exercising their faith and were excluded from education. In addition, they were not allowed to teach or even speak themselves.

Separate outer court for women

The tabernacle and the first temple built by Solomon had a holy place (the Holy of Holies) and an outer court where both men and women were allowed to go. But Herod's new temple had an extra outer court for women and heathens. Women were not allowed to go further than their own separate court. This kept them even further away from the most holy place. Presumably the women were also kept separate in the synagogues on closed-off balconies.

Women were barely taught the Law

When God made a covenant with Moses and gave him laws and regulations for the people, women were part of that as well. Because in Deuteronomy Moses said: "All of you are standing today in the presence of the Lord your God – your leaders and chief men, your elders and officials, and all the other men of Israel, together with your children and your wives, and the foreigners living in your camps… You are standing here in order to enter into a covenant with the Lord your God."[38] Later on Moses said: "Assemble the people – men, women and children, and the foreigners residing in your towns – so they can listen and learn to fear the Lord your God and follow carefully all the words of this law."[39]

If Moses stated so clearly that women were to be included and should be instructed in the Law, then how could the Jews later say that it was no longer allowed?

According to the famous rabbi Hillel,[40] the grandfather of Gamaliel, it was a waste of time to teach a girl the Law because a totally unknowledgeable person cannot become a saint. Yet later on Gamaliel educated his own daughter. However, that was an exception to the rule.

Rabbi Eliezer, one of the most prominent wise men of the first and second century in Judea and a contemporary of Gamaliel, thought that a man should not teach his daughter the knowledge of the Law. It was as if you were teaching her to be sacrilegious, he declared.

מאימתי פרק ראשון ברכות ב

Page from the Berakhot tractate. In the center and underneath the decorated box is the text of the Mishnah, followed by the Gemara. Around it are comments from important medieval scholars.

From their viewpoint it was logical that women did not need to be taught, as they were not allowed to do anything with their knowledge anyway! And when you read what Paul said in 1 Corinthians 14:34, it would seem that he agreed with that:

Women should remain silent in the churches. They are not allowed to speak, but must be in submission, as the law says.

But if we are to take these words of Paul as a general law that women should be silent, what then are we to do about the Bible verses that say that women can prophesy? In his first letter to the Corinthians, Paul said that women who pray or prophesy (speak on behalf of God to an individual or a group of people) should not do so without a head covering: "Every man who prays or prophesies with his head covered dishonors his head. But every woman who prays or prophesies with her head uncovered dishonors her head – it is the same as having her head shaved."[41] So it seems they *are* allowed to speak.

We read here that women should cover their head **when they pray or prophesy**, but in the churches in which women are still expected to wear a hat, they are not usually allowed to pray or prophesy. Yet they wear a hat during the entire service. That is like wearing a helmet even though you are not even on a motorcycle.

You can also question where the idea of hats came from, because just a few verses later Paul said that women received their long hair as a covering: "… but that if a woman has long hair, it is her glory? For long hair is given to her as a covering."[42]

Speaking of hats...

Some churches require women to wear a hat during the service. Whatever your thoughts are on that, wearing a hat is also a cultural expression. For, after all, if it was a rule for all ages, then why do we see women wearing a hat in some churches, yet the men there do not pray with uplifted hands? Because that was the requirement for men. Throughout the ages, men wore hats, especially in Western nations. Wigs (in the era of wigs), bowler hats, cowboy hats and today baseball caps have been the popular choice. Yet the hat as a fashion item has pretty much disappeared since the sixties.

There have always been female prophets who spoke to people (both men and women) on behalf of God. We have already mentioned the prophetess Huldah,[43] and in the New Testament we read about the prophetess Anna. She prophesied over Jesus in the temple.[44] The prophet Isaiah was married to a prophetess.[45] The four daughters of Philip prophesied.[46] On the day of Pentecost, when the Holy Spirit was poured out, Peter quoted the prophet Joel, who had announced years earlier that women would also prophesy. Speaking on behalf of God is for sons *and* daughters, for manservants *and* maidservants.[47]

In short, Paul cannot have meant that all women should always be silent when he said that women should remain silent in the church. So what did he mean? We will get back to that later on. For now, it is important that you realize that Greek, Roman and Jewish women were not allowed to speak out. Women had to be submissive to their husbands and could not be in leadership roles. A man was allowed to decide his wife's fate. If he spotted a beautiful woman – often just a young girl –it was quite normal for him to have her brought to him to fulfill his needs and serve him: as a wife, a concubine or a slave girl. She was his possession. According to the traditions

Anna prophesied over Jesus in the temple.

of Mishnah, he had the legal right to divorce her if he wanted. A woman did not have that right. She was not allowed to divorce her husband.[48]

In short, women were in bad circumstances in the Jewish culture when Jesus came, but it is not our primary goal to talk about that. We are merely sketching out the cultural situation of that time so that you can see how special and radically different Jesus was in all those areas, and Paul who followed in His footsteps. Then you will discover God's heart for women.

CHAPTER 4

HOW DOES GOD VIEW WOMEN?

At the beginning of the Bible we can see that God viewed women very differently from the ancient Greeks, Romans and Jews. According to the Greeks and Romans, women were a curse for men, but when God created Eve, He called her a valuable helper for Adam. He said: "It is not good for the man to be alone. I will make a **helper** (*êzer*, H5828) suitable for him." Then God put Adam into a deep sleep and took one of his ribs from his body. He formed a woman out of it and brought her to Adam.[49]

This word "helper" does not mean that Eve is some kind of inferior servant to Adam. The Bible uses the same word, *êzer*, again and again when it speaks of God's own powerful assistance (help) to people, usually in military situations.[50] Look at Psalm 33:20, for example:

"We wait in hope for the Lord; **he is our help** and our shield." After this was discovered, the meaning of *êzer* was expanded to signify "powerful help". The word *êzer* is also used to commemorate God's deliverance of the people of Israel. When Samuel looked back at Israel's victories, he built a monument of stone and named it Eben-Haëzer to remind Israel that the Lord had helped them at that point.[51] In short, the woman is a powerful, enabling helper for the man; a warrior.

Here is an interesting detail: the fact that God created Eve from Adam's rib is proof that men and women have the same origin; something they did not believe in Greek culture. That Eve and Adam had the same origin was also proved when Adam later on said: "This is now bone of my bones and flesh of my flesh." The woman does not have another origin, inferior to that of her husband, as the Greeks thought.

God viewed the woman as a valuable helper for the man, just as He calls Himself a valuable helper. Very different from the Greeks, Romans and Jews, who compared the value of women with that of possessions, just as you can own slaves or animals.

When a man wants a woman, she is taken from her parental home. Men traditionally were used to having one or more women if they wanted. It was not the men but the women who had to give up everything. Abraham, for example, sent a servant to his birthplace to pick up a wife for his son Isaac. That was never how God meant it to be. The Bible says exactly the opposite in Genesis. According to God, the *man* is the one who should leave his parental home for his wife! He is to give up everything for her. That is the total opposite:

That is why a man leaves his father and mother and is united to his wife, and they become one flesh.[52]

Men, love your wives

Centuries later, Paul revived God's original intention. He reminded the men of Ephesus of God's words in Genesis 2:24: "That is why a man leaves his father and mother and is united to his wife, and they become one flesh." In Ephesus in those days men ruled over their wives, but Paul has a powerful message for them.[53] He sharply corrects them, as he speaks mostly to the men and commands them to be in *mutual submission*. Living by the Spirit means that a man cannot act like the boss, but that he has responsibilities toward his wife. Husbands must love their wives, even if it costs them their lives. Paul compares this to Christ, who gave Himself completely for the church. That is the way husbands should treat their wives. Not as if they were property, which they can take into their home and whose their fate they can determine when and how they want, but as their precious partners, for whom they leave everything in order to be with them and to be faithful to them.

Men and women rule together over the animals, but not over each other

When God first spoke about the people He wanted to create, He had it in mind that they would rule over creation together. He said: "Let us make mankind in our image, in our likeness, so that they may rule over the fish in the sea and the birds in the sky, over the livestock and all the wild animals, and over all the creatures that move along the ground."[54] God created people in His image, male and female. God blessed them and said to them: "Be fruitful and increase in number; fill the earth and subdue it. Rule over the fish in the sea and the birds in the sky and over every living creature that moves on the ground."[55]

God gave men and woman an equal role. Yet, a few chapters later, God said: "Your desire will be for your husband, and **he will rule over you.**"[56]

What had happened in the meantime, so that man had now become the ruler? Sin had entered the world! Adam and Eve ate the fruit of the tree of knowledge of good and evil. That caused a curse to come upon creation. God confronted Adam and Eve with the unavoidable consequences of their disobedience. One of these is that men will rule over women. This was not God's will, but a result of sin entering the world. God's heart for women is still for them to be treated as equals by men, and not to be regarded as women to be ruled over, even though this still happens today as a result of the fall of humankind.

God did not curse humankind. He did curse the snake (the devil) and the earth,[57] but He foretold that Jesus would come to destroy the devil. There was hope right away! God already had His plan of salvation worked out. "He said to the serpent: And I will put enmity between you and the woman, and between your seed and her

Seed; He shall bruise your head, and you shall bruise His heel."[58] (NKJV) Jesus is called the seed of the *woman* here, not of the man. What a big contrast (again!) with the Greeks, who thought that babies were completely developed from men's seed, and that women were no part of that. They merely provided the safe environment (the womb) in which the baby could grow. This idea was the norm for many centuries; it was not until halfway through the 19th century that it became clear that both male and female cells are needed for conception.

So we see that from the very beginning God viewed women differently, with regard to their origin, their value and their destiny. And in spite of that we also see that it went wrong almost immediately, following the fall of humankind. Maybe you have started to dislike the condescending attitude toward women that you have noted in the chapters on the Greeks, Romans and Jews. But make no mistake: you also see this in the Bible, in the lives of people who are known as heroes of the faith. In Genesis we see that Abraham, Isaac and Jacob did not deal with women the way God intended. Abraham took Sarah's slave Hagar as his concubine and got her pregnant (which happened to be Sarah's idea, by the way), while God's intention for marriage was that each man should have his own wife and remain faithful to her. Isaac took Rebecca to comfort himself: he slept with her in the tent of his mother. After that he loved her and she became his wife. Jacob wanted to marry Rachel but was given Leah; then he married Rachel anyway. He had children with both wives as well as with two concubines.

Ladies first

In Judges 13 we read about a man named Manoah. He was married to a woman who is not mentioned by name. They wanted children, but his wife was infertile. Then an angel of God appeared and told her that she would become pregnant. He gave her instructions not to drink wine or eat anything unclean, because her son would be dedicated to the Lord as a Nazirite from the womb. He would commence the deliverance of Israel from the hands of the Philistines. She was excited and told her husband what the angel had said. Manoah fervently sought God and asked if the angel could appear once more. This does happen; the angel appeared to the woman while she was in the field and her husband was not there. She went to get her husband and this time the angel also spoke to Manoah. Manoah asked the angel what his name was and the angel answered: "Why do you ask my name? It is beyond understanding." Then the angel did something amazing: he ascended in the flame of the altar. Manoah thought they would surely die, because they had seen God, but his wife remained full of faith. "If God had wanted to kill us, then He would not have given us such promises", she said to him. Sometime later she gave birth to a son and named him… Samson.

It is quite exceptional how God visited this infertile woman, in a culture in which women had an inferior status – *especially* if they were childless. God spoke to the woman first through the angel, and later He also spoke to her husband. This woman had such incredible faith as she pointed out God's promises to her husband when he was afraid. She exceeded her husband in faith.

Years later also Mary (the mother of Jesus) and Elizabeth (the mother of John the Baptist) both received a visit from an angel when their husbands were not present.

CHAPTER 5

HOW JESUS TREATED WOMEN

In the Gospels we see a big change taking place. Jesus brought in a new era. He brought to earth God's Kingdom, in which everything was different from the ruling cultures of the Greeks, Romans and Jews of those days. Radically different. Jesus brought good news for all people: for the lost, the sick, the weak, the poor, the demon-possessed – and for the women. The way Jesus treated women was unheard of in those days and went against all of the prevailing beliefs and rules.

Female disciples followed Jesus, and Jesus allowed it
From the very beginning of Jesus' ministry there were women following Him. As He started to travel around to preach the good news of the Kingdom, the twelve disci-

ples went with Him and also several women, as Luke noted. They were not used to this, as women normally did not travel with men.

Later on, we read that he was talking about a group of people. Of course, this group of people needed to eat and it was women who covered their expenses. That too was very uncommon in those days, that a man would allow himself to be cared for financially by a woman. Luke mentioned these women by name and also shared a bit about their background. Mary Magdalene was a woman who had been possessed by seven demons (Jesus obviously had no problems with her past). This Mary Magdalene was also present during the death and burial of Jesus and she was the first person to see Him after He rose from the dead. When she recognized the risen Jesus, she cried out: "Rabboni"[59] That means Master. Mary did not just travel with Jesus; she was a student of the school of Rabbi Jesus and was privileged to have more than the average opportunities to hear His teaching, to talk to Him and to see Him at work. In those days, women did not study under rabbis and it was inappropriate for a woman to travel with a rabbi.

Mary Magdalene was the first to witness Jesus' resurrection.

Mary, apostle of the apostles

In 591 Pope Gregory claimed that Mary Magdalene was a prostitute, but in 2016 Mary Magdalene was officially recognized as an apostle of the apostles and the first messenger of the risen Jesus.[60]

Another woman who, according to Luke, was one of Jesus' followers, was Joanna. She was the wife of Chuza, the manager of the household of Herod, who was wealthy and ruled over Galilee. As his manager, Chuza would undoubtedly have had a good salary, so Joanna was a wealthy lady. Then there was Susanna, of whom nothing more is known. There were many others who helped support Jesus out of their own means.[61]

Interesting detail: the Greek word that has been translated as "supported" is διακονέω. In Strong's Concordance it says the following:

diakoneō

dee-ak-on-eh'-o

From G1249; to be an attendant, that is, wait upon (menially or as a host, friend or [figuratively] teacher); technically to act as a Christian deacon: - (ad-) minister (unto), serve, use the office of a deacon.

So Jesus already had female deacons (servant leaders) who also provided for Him financially.

When Jesus went to Golgotha, there were women surrounding Him as well. When Jesus was led away with a cross on His back to the location where He would be crucified, He was followed by a large crowd. Among them were several women, who were mourning loudly. Jesus turned and spoke to them: "Daughters of Jerusalem, do not cry for me," and He explained to them what would happen in the future. It was extremely unusual to speak to women like this in public![62]

Women joined Joseph of Arimathea on a visit to Jesus' grave to prepare spices and myrrh for His body.[63] The disciples on the road to Emmaus spoke about the women in their group[64] who had gone to the grave early in the morning and seen angels there, who told them that Jesus was alive. There were also women present in the upper room: Mary, the mother of Jesus, and other women.[65] Jesus had commanded them to wait there for the promise from the Father.

Jesus is being taken to Calvary where they will crucify Him. Only Luke describes the meeting with the women.

In everything Jesus did, it was clear that He did not distinguish between men and women, and He said this as well: "All those the Father gives me will come to me, and whoever comes to me I will never drive away."[66] Jesus welcomed everyone, men and women. Even sinful women, as you can read in the following story.

One day the Jews came to Jesus with a woman who had been caught in the act of adultery. They were trying to tempt Jesus so that they would have a reason to prosecute Him. They pointed out the law to Jesus, which commanded that adulterous women should be stoned. Where is the man in all this, you may wonder? According to the law of Moses, he was to be killed too![67] But the man was not important to the Jews in this story. Jewish scholars had added to their books that it was lawful for a man to commit adultery. According to them, the man had not committed an offense.

Jesus did not play the Jews' little game. He did not give them a direct answer to their question (indeed, He rarely did), but He pointedly made them think about their own consciences. They were probably not used to that.

The day after the Sabbath, the women go to the grave with their herbs and fragrant spices to care for the body of Jesus. The angel tells them that He has risen.

But Jesus bent down and started to write on the ground with his finger. When they kept on questioning him, he straightened up and said to them, "Let any one of you who is without sin be the first to throw a stone at her." Again, he stooped down and wrote on the ground. At this, those who heard began to go away one at a time, the older ones first, until only Jesus was left, with the woman still standing there. Jesus straightened up and asked her, "Woman, where are they? Has no one condemned you?" "No one, sir," she said. "Then neither do I condemn you," Jesus declared. "Go now and leave your life of sin."[68]

Jesus called a woman forward in the synagogue

As we mentioned previously, women were not allowed to go to the front of the temple, so they probably did not go to the front of the synagogue either. There were separate places behind a screen for them, but Jesus did not care about that, because when He was teaching on a Sabbath in the synagogue, He saw a woman who was bent over by a demonic illness. He called her up to Him and said to her: "Woman, you are set free from your infirmity."[69] Jesus called the woman up to the front so that everyone could see her. He not only healed her, but He called her a daughter of Abraham too; an heir of Abraham. This was unheard of because in the rabbinical writings only Jewish men were called sons of Abraham.

Inheritance laws for women

The Jewish laws stipulated that only men could inherit when their father died. If a man had no sons, his inheritance went to his brothers; daughters were passed over. In Numbers 27 we read how God changed the law so that women could inherit if their father had no sons. We read how a certain man named Zelophehad had died, leaving no sons. But He did have five daughters. They went to Moses and said: "Why should our father's name disappear just because he did not have a son? Give us property among our father's relatives." Moses brought the matter before God and God said the women were right. He said to Moses: "You must certainly give them property as an inheritance among their father's relatives and give their father's inheritance to them." Then God said that the Israelites needed to change their laws: "If a man dies and leaves no son, give his inheritance to his daughter. If he has no daughter, give his inheritance to his brothers. If he has no brothers, give his inheritance to his father's brothers. If his father had no brothers, give his inheritance to the nearest relative in his clan, that he may possess it. This is to have the force of law for the Israelites, as the Lord commanded Moses."[70] The laws of Israel were changed on the spot when women asked for it, because God does not exclude women.

Later we see that Jesus even apparently changed His attitude when a woman appealed to Him. Jesus did not want to focus on the Gentiles for He had come primarily for "the lost sheep of the house of Israel", but when a Canaanite woman kept asking Him for help, Jesus changed His mind and healed her daughter. He listened to her.[71]

Jesus restores God's original plan for marriage
Jesus also protested the law that said men were allowed to divorce their wives. When a few Jewish men tried to get Jesus to react on this issue, He pointed them to God's original intention for marriage in which men and women are equal. You can read this story in Matthew 19:

Some Pharisees came to him to test him. They asked, "Is it lawful for a man to divorce his wife for any and every reason?" "Haven't you read," he replied, "that at the beginning the Creator 'made them male and female,' and said, 'For this reason a man will leave his father and mother and be united to his wife, and the two will become one flesh'? So, they are no longer two, but one flesh. Therefore, what God has joined together, let no one separate. "Why then," they asked, "did Moses command that a man give his wife a certificate of divorce and send her away?" Jesus replied, "Moses permitted you to divorce your wives because your hearts were hard. But it was not this way from the beginning. I tell you that anyone who divorces his wife, except for sexual immorality, and marries another woman commits adultery." The disciples said to him, "If this is the situation between a husband and wife, it is better not to marry." Jesus replied, "Not everyone can accept this word, but only those to whom it has been given."[72]

This occurrence was also noted by Mark, with a small addition that proves that Jesus did not distinguish between men and women when it came to marital rights and duties. He said to these Jewish people: "Anyone who divorces his wife and marries another woman commits adultery against her. And if she divorces her husband and marries another man, she commits adultery."[73]

The disciples probably had to swallow hard when they heard this, because they too had grown up in a culture that was not used to giving women the same rights as men. We see that divorce was never God's heart for people, even though it does still happen.

Jesus is the Son of man

The most beautiful proof that Jesus cares about both men and women is probably the fact that He frequently called Himself the Son of man, as in humankind. He came not only for men, but also for women. In the Jewish, as well as the Greek and Roman, culture, it was very important to be a man, but Jesus restored women in value, position and ministry.

Jesus spoke to women

According to the Talmud,[74] it was forbidden for a man to speak to a woman. But Jesus did speak to them. He even spoke to non-Jewish women, which was highly unusual in those days. In John 4, a Samaritan woman says to Him: "You are a Jew and I am a Samaritan woman. How can you ask me for a drink?" and then a comment is added: "(For Jews do not associate with Samaritans.)"[75] Many Jewish leaders even tried to avoid *looking* at women. It was no wonder, then, that the disciples were surprised that Jesus was speaking to one, and a foreign one to boot.[76]

Actually it should not surprise us, when we are seeking to discern God's heart for women, that we see that God has no trouble speaking to a woman. Not even when she is a foreign slave girl, like Hagar, the second wife of Abraham and the mother of Ishmael. When Hagar fled Sarah's humiliation, God watched out for her and He sent an angel of the Lord (often an expression for God Himself) to talk to her and encourage her. Hagar returned because God commanded her to do so, but later she was sent away by Abraham. Thirsty and sad, she wandered through the desert, and once again an angel of God came to her to encourage her and help her.[77] This is a beautiful expression of God's heart for women. His heart was powerfully expressed centuries later by Paul, when he said that God does not distinguish between people: there is neither Jew nor Gentile, neither slave nor free, nor is there male and female; it does not matter to God.[78]

Another woman who was ostracized by society was the one with an "issue of blood".[79] She had been bleeding for over twelve years. According to the purification laws of

Moses,[80] this woman was unclean. She had to live separately from other people, because if she touched them they too would become unclean. It is understandable that she was terrified when she finally admitted that she was the one who had touched Jesus. But, instead of condemning her, Jesus praised her for her faith!

Separated in a hut

Jesus showed that menstruation was no longer an apparent source of impurity and that women no longer need to separate themselves off – although that still happens in some cultures. In Nepal women are banished to an old hut or cowshed during menstruation, as, according to an old Hindu tradition (*chhaupadi*), they are considered unclean. No one is allowed to touch them, because then they too become unclean. This separation is not only uncomfortable for women, it is also dangerous. The huts are not usually insulated, so during the cold Nepali winters it freezes inside. In late 2019 at least one woman died of smoke inhalation because she was trying to heat her hut with a fire. The huts also have no sanitary facilities, which are very important, especially during menstruation. Girls and women

Jesus spoke to the Samaritan woman. A painting by Angelica Kauffman (1796).

usually only get a cloth to use for their period, and banishment to a hut can give rise to serious conditions such as diarrhea, dehydration, hypothermia and even snake bite. They are also very vulnerable to rape. They are far away from everyone who could help them. Officially, *chhaupadi* has been forbidden since 2005, but in the western Himalayan region it is still a custom.

"In a society in which women
only counted if they gave birth
to children, Jesus gave
them a new perspective."

CHAPTER 6

WOMEN WHO SERVED JESUS

Leadership was a job for men that was culturally determined. Even though there were examples in the Bible of female leadership, such as Deborah and Miriam, they still were an exception.

Deborah, an exceptionally gifted, female leader

In Judges we read about Deborah. She was the leader not of a church, but of an entire nation! In addition to that, she was a prophetess and she wrote a portion of the book of Judges. Peter said the following about the authors of the Bible: "Above all, you must understand that no prophecy of Scripture came about by the prophet's own interpretation of things. For prophecy never had its origin in the human will, but prophets, though human, spoke from God as they were carried along by the Holy Spirit."[81] Deborah was therefore a holy woman of God, who was guided by the Holy Spirit when she wrote a portion of the Bible.

At the time of Jesus, we not only see more female leadership; we even see that Jesus empowered and released women in this leadership. Leadership has always been connected to serving. When we read in Acts that seven men were chosen to lead the church, Luke uses the word *diakonia* (G1247).[82] In this case they were men, but the role of diakonia was not limited to men alone. There are various examples of women who served Jesus, and the same word diakonia, is used to describe their work.[83] We can see from this that there were both male and female deacons (leaders); literally: people who served others.

However, it was quite remarkable that women served in this capacity. An aspect of Jewish culture at the time was that women could not serve God independently. According to the rabbis, women could do this only indirectly, through their husband or son. They were also not equipped for ministry, because only boys and men studied the scriptures in the synagogue. The only goal for a woman was to have children and raise them. If you were childless in those days, you had no value. Jesus showed us that He had very different thoughts on the matter. Just take a look at the following situation.

When Jesus was speaking to his followers one day, a woman in the crowd spontaneously cried out: "Blessed is the mother who gave you birth and nursed you." In other words: your mother is a happy woman! Jesus answered in a curious manner: "Blessed rather are those who hear the word of God and obey it."[84]

Why did Jesus say this? Because He wanted to give women a new perspective. You are more blessed when you receive the word of God, or, in other words: you will be happier as a woman – with or without children – if you accept teaching and live the kind of life that God wants. That may be as a person in leadership or as a teacher. Jesus threw out all the Jewish ideas on the purpose of women in one go. In a society in which women counted only if they gave birth to children, He gave them a new perspective. It was the crowning glory for a woman (as well as a man) to be a disciple of Jesus. That is where one's true identity lies.

Ave Maria

In the Roman-Catholic Hail Mary (Latin: *Ave Maria*), a prayer directed to the Holy Virgin Mary, the mother of Jesus, Mary's intercession is requested. The prayer starts with the blessing that Elizabeth (the mother of John the Baptist) spoke when Mary came to visit her while carrying the baby Jesus in her womb: "Hail Mary, full of grace, the Lord is with thee. Blessed are thou among women, and blessed is the fruit of thy womb, Jesus." This prayer is in line with a culture that dictated that you were blessed as a woman if you bore children. Mary may have been declared a saint because she was the mother of Jesus. But Elizabeth had a greater understanding, because she adding something else to her spontaneous blessing of Mary, which was totally in line with Jesus' reaction to the spontaneous cry of the woman in Luke 11: "Blessed is she who has believed that the Lord would fulfill his promises to her!" Mary is blessed not just because she is the mother of Jesus, but also because she believed what God told her.

Madonna and child, embroidered bij Frédérique Moussault.

Blessed are you (as a woman) if you get an education. Women generally did not receive an education, as we just saw. Jesus did not agree with that custom. When He taught, there were women present and listening as well. Many Jewish leaders thought this was improper and even scandalous.

Jesus did much of His teaching outside the temple, in the villages; He might have done this because there were no temple walls there to separate the men from the women. And when He did speak in the temple, He did it in locations where women were also allowed to be present: in the temple courts where the offerings were placed, and in the temple courts in Solomon's Colonnade.[85]

In Jewish culture the home was also a place where people were educated in the scriptures, but, according to the traditional Mishnah (commentary on the Torah by Jewish scholars) this was forbidden for women. Luke describes Paul lying at the feet of his teacher.[86] "Lying at someone's feet" was the usual way of indicating that a person was receiving teaching. That Paul was lying at the feet of Gamaliel meant that Paul was his student.

Jesus teaches Mary, but Martha struggles with that. A painting by Tintoretto (16th century).

Luke describes how Mary was lying at the feet of Jesus in exactly the same manner. Just in her home. That meant that she was being taught by Him! Her sister, Martha, was upset that Mary was sitting at Jesus' feet as if she were his student, and asked Jesus to put her in her place. But Jesus did not do that. He directly ignored the prohibition on teaching women and explained why it was so important: teaching by Jesus, the Word, cannot be taken from you. According to Jesus, Mary "chose what was better".[87] The fact that Jesus used the word "chose" is also quite significant. Women did not have much choice in those days. It was an incredible empowerment for Mary and the women who came after her. For if you receive education it means you can *give* education.

Mary had listened very carefully to the teachings of Jesus

When Jesus announces (four times) that he is going to suffer and die, his disciples do not believe him. Mary does believe Him, because when she later anoints Jesus with precious oils and wipes His feet with her hair, Jesus tells those present in the house that she had carefully saved these oils in preparation for His funeral.

Jesus taught not only Mary, but also other women. He took time to explain things about the resurrection to Martha when her brother, Lazarus, had died. He taught her that people will not die if they believe in Him and told her the secret: "I am the resurrection and the life. The one who believes in me will live, even though they die; and whoever lives by believing in me will never die. Do you believe this?" "Yes, Lord," she replied, "I believe that you are the Messiah, the Son of God, who is to come into the world."[88] That must have been a special moment for Martha.

Jesus had a conversation with a Samaritan woman at a well, where He taught her. [89] This is the longest registered conversation in the Bible that Jesus had with a woman, and not just any woman at that: as a Samaritan rejected by the Jews, as a woman rejected by men, and as a sinner rejected by other women. Jesus did not reject her, however, quite the opposite: He took her very seriously. She was one of the first people Jesus told that He was the Messiah.

The Samaritan woman was so impressed by her meeting with Jesus that she left her water jug and ran back to the village to tell other people about Jesus. The first evangelist was a woman! And Jesus did not stop her. She was allowed to tell others about Jesus and share what He taught her, with both men and women.

Later Jesus told all His disciples to go out, share the gospel and baptize everyone.[90] This applied to all believers. He also called on women to teach the gospel. It is logical that women should receive teaching, for how would they be able to share something if they had not first learned it themselves?

Something to think about

If women were not allowed to teach men, then why is Mary's Song recorded in the Bible?[91] And what should we do about the teaching of King Lemuel? In Proverbs 31 he taught about women just as his mother had taught him: that is what it says. He obtained his teaching from a woman! We cannot ignore the teaching of this woman, because Paul says that *all* scripture is God-breathed and useful for teaching.[92] Yet King Lemuel's mother remains partially anonymous.

Henrietta Mears

Henrietta Mears (1890–1963) remained largely unknown as well; you have probably never heard of her. But everyone knows of Billy Graham, the best-known evangelist of the 20th century. He passed away in 2018, aged 99. Henrietta Mears was Billy Graham's great inspiration. He said the following about her: "She has had a remarkable influence on my life, both directly and indirectly. I doubt that another woman other than my wife and mother has had such a clear influence. Her graceful spirit, her devoted life, her steadfastness for the simple gospel and her knowledge of the Bible have been a constant source of inspiration for me. She is one of the greatest Christians I have ever known."[93]

Henrietta was one of the most influential Bible teachers of the 20th century. In addition to Billy Graham, she has also had a major influence on Bill Bright (founder of Campus Crusade for Christ) and Dawson Trotman (founder of the Navigators). She equipped an incredible number of young Christian leaders and set up a Sunday-school curriculum for children and adults. Under

Henrietta Mears: "Never say: I'm just a Sunday school teacher."

her leadership, the Sunday school grew from four hundred and fifty to more than four thousand students a week. Her Bible study material was published in many languages and her book *What the Bible is All About* was a bestseller in 1953. She was proud that she could serve the Lord with her gifts and took her task extremely seriously, convinced that God had called her to it. One of her statements was: "Never say: 'I'm just a Sunday school teacher'. If you were a professor at Harvard or Oxford, you would be proud – proud of the great responsibility. As a Sunday-school teacher, you can be just as proud; not the kind of pride that lifts itself, but the warm, happy feeling of satisfaction that you get when you serve the Lord. What a responsibility do you have to teach an immortal soul to have intimacy with God! To fulfill this responsibility, you must be fully committed to the Lord and the task He gives you. Christ was a teacher. He told you and me that it is our mission to teach (Matthew 28:19, 20). So never say: I am only a Sunday-school teacher, because you are a teacher at the University of Christ!"[94]

"It was quite normal for Paul
to recognize women in their
God-given spiritual position."

CHAPTER 7

FEMALE LEADERS AT THE TIME OF PAUL

Paul was helped by a couple named Priscilla and Aquila when founding churches in Corinth, Ephesus and Rome. He calls them his fellow laborers in Christ and he is very grateful to them, because they even risked their lives for him.[95] Priscilla and Aquila are always mentioned together in the Bible and usually Priscilla's name is listed first.[96] That was very unusual in those days, as the man was always named first.

It would seem that Priscilla had even more of a leadership role in the teaching of Apollos. They took him home and explained all that had happened to Jesus and what that meant.[97] Priscilla's student grew to be an important leader in the early church in Achaia, where he was used by God in a powerful manner to support the Christians there.[98]

Even the fourth century church father John Chrysostom, who was known for his many derogatory statements about women, recognizes that Paul mentioned Priscilla before her husband because he probably saw more fruit from her than from him. Another church father, Tertullian, claims that the saint Prisca (Priscilla) preached the gospel. That is quite remarkable, because this Tertullian was also known for his accusatory remarks about women. According to him, they were the gateway to the devil, violators of the divine law, destroyers of God's image.

In Acts we read an amazing story in which we see that it is quite normal for Paul to acknowledge women in their God-given spiritual position. He also has no issues with explaining the gospel to women. The story starts when Paul has a vision at night in which a Macedonian man beckons him and says: "Come over and help us". This man is an image of the entire people of Macedonia (in present-day Greece). Paul understood that God wanted them to go to Macedonia – not to meet this man but to preach the gospel to the entire Macedonian people – and the next day he and his associates crossed the water to Macedonia. They finally arrived in Philippi. They didn't know where to start. They had been in the city for a few days and, on the Sabbath, they decided to take a walk to a place outside the city where prayer usually took place. They sat down and talked to the women who had gathered there to pray. These were women who served God.[99]

Let's think about this. Paul and a group of companions visit different congregations to encourage them, are blocked from going one way by the Holy Spirit and are sent in another direction by means of a vision. He abruptly changes his plans and leaves for Macedonia, undoubtedly with high expectations, because a vision from God is no small thing. How different things are upon arrival, though. The Macedonian people are not waiting for them with open arms and they do not seem to need any help. Instead, they meet a group of women who are praying. Was Paul disappointed? We do not know. We do know that God was building a bridge through these women for Paul to start a great work in Macedonia.

One of the women at this place of prayer was Lydia, a seller of purple: an entrepreneur. God opened her heart and she received Paul's teaching. She was saved and her house became the center of the ministry that God started through Paul in Philippi. The first Macedonian who came to faith was a woman. We know how the story ends: because Paul freed a girl from a spirit of divination, he and Silas were thrown into prison. They praised God there and were released from prison by an earthquake. The jailer and his family came to faith through this wonderful event. This is how the congregation began in Philippi, to which Paul later writes letters. It is a very special church, and because they were so grateful that Paul had brought them the gospel they supported him financially. In the beginning they were the only ones to do that.[100]

In the time of Paul, the church was mainly organized into house churches. Paul regularly wrote letters to the leaders of these churches to support and encourage them spiritually. He also sent greetings to the various house churches that were there, to both the leaders and the church members. He always did that in pretty much the same way:

Romans 16:10b *Greet those who belong to the* **household** *of Aristobulus.11b Greet those in the* **household** *of Narcissus who are in the Lord.*

1 Corinthians 1:16 *Yes, I also baptized the* **household** *of Stephanas; beyond that, I don't remember if I baptized anyone else.*

1 Corinthians 16:19 *The churches in the province of Asia send you greetings. Aquila and Priscilla greet you warmly in the Lord, and so does the church that meets at their* **house***.*

Romans 16:3-5 *Greet Priscilla and Aquila, my co-workers in Christ Jesus. They risked their lives for me. Not only I but all the churches of the Gentiles are grateful to them. Greet also the church that meets at their* **house***.*

2 Timothy 1:16 *May the Lord show mercy to the* **household** *of Onesiphorus, because he often refreshed me and was not ashamed of my chains.*

2 Timothy 4:19 *Greet Priscilla and Aquila and the* **household** *of Onesiphorus.*

Paul used the same wording to describe the house of Chloë. She too was a leader of one of the house churches in Corinth:

1 Corinthians 1:11 *My brothers and sisters, some from Chloë's* **household** *have informed me that there are quarrels among you.*

There were women who led house churches as well. A few Bible translators believe that Nympha was a woman, but not all agree; the King James Version says that Nympha was a man. Most other translations, however, say that Nympha was a woman.

Colossians 4:15 *Give my greetings to the brothers and sisters at Laodicea, and to Nympha and the church in her* **house***.*

As regards our question of whether women too could be leaders in Paul's time, it does not really matter whether Nympha was a woman or a man. Chloë was certainly a woman. Conclusion: the "home-church leader" position could therefore also be filled by a woman.

In his letters Paul mentions 39 colleagues in ministry, including ten women.[101] He makes no distinction between men and women. For example, he asks the members of the congregation in Philippi to help Euodia and Syntyche: women who, according to Paul, fought together with him for the gospel, along with Clement and his other fellow workers.[102]

Paul regarded women as allies in the battle to spread the gospel. But Euodia and Syntyche had had a disagreement that kept them from their duties and threatened the church. Although Paul wanted to correct them and build them up, it is not his intention to humiliate the women. On the contrary: between the lines we read that they must have meant a lot to him, because they had fought alongside him. He apparently appreciated them just as much as he did Clement and his other co-laborers. Men and women are indispensable in the fight.

Paul also talks about Junia, who was probably a female apostle (although some Bible translators believe that Junia was a man).[103]

Phoebe, a special woman and a leader

In the letter to the Romans we are introduced to Phoebe,[104] a woman who was connected to the Christian church in Cenchreae, a harbor city to the east of

Paul greatly respected Phoebe, a deacon of the church in Cenchreae.

Corinth. She was sent by Paul as a delegate from the church to Rome, to deliver his letter to the Romans, and he recommends her highly: "I commend to you our sister Phoebe, a deacon of the church in Cenchreae. I ask you to receive her in the Lord in a way worthy of his people and to give her any help she may need from you, for she has been the benefactor of many people, including me."

Paul calls her a *prostatis* (G4368), translated as "benefactor". As a noun this occurs only once in the New Testament, but we find derivative forms of this word in places where it is translated as "leadership" (Romans 12: 8; 1 Thessalonians 5:12).[105]

When Paul calls on the Romans to receive her in a worthy manner, we know that he must have meant with much respect for her. When teaching Timothy, he explained that we must have great respect for good leaders in the church, especially those who work for the word and teach the doctrine.[106] Here, too, the Greek word for "leadership" is a derivative of the word *prostatis*.

All this shows how strong Paul's recommendation of Phoebe was: according to him, she was an extraordinary sister, deacon and leader. The Romans were probably not used to such a recommendation at that time!

CHAPTER 8

I DO NOT PERMIT A WOMAN TO TEACH

"I do not permit a woman to teach or to assume authority over a man; she must be quiet."

One of the most "difficult" verses on women in ministry comes in the first letter from Paul to Timothy: "I do not permit a woman to teach or to assume authority over a man; she must be quiet."[107]

Paul was encouraging his younger pupil Timothy to be a good servant of Christ. Timothy had been appointed as a pastor and leader of the church in Ephesus.[108] When Paul wrote his letter to Timothy, Ephesus had for about 100 years been part of the Roman empire, where we have seen that woman had more say in matters than before. There were all kinds of things going on in the church. There were false teachers spreading heresy and there was fighting going on, with both men and women involved. Timothy had the noble task of dealing with the heresy and confronting and silencing the ones who were spreading it.

Paul gave Timothy instructions on what he had to teach the members of the church.[109] The most important thing was that there was to be intercession by all people. Paul wrote first to the men and then to the women with specific instructions on how they should pray. Men were to pray with holy, uplifted hands, without anger or dispute. Then he gave regulations on how women were to pray. Ephesus was an immoral city and wearing pearls was considered immodest behavior. Women were therefore to pray with modesty of manner and dress: "I also want the women to dress modestly, with decency and propriety, adorning themselves, not with elaborate hairstyles or gold or pearls or expensive clothes, but with good deeds, appropriate for women who profess to worship God."[110]

Why was modest clothing so important? Because he was talking about women who were in ministry! We can deduce that from the words Paul uses when he says "appropriate for women who **profess** to worship God".

This word "profess" (G1861) is one of the seven words for communication that Paul uses in his letters. They are all derived from the Greek word *agello* (messenger). Here in 1 Timothy 2:10 he uses the word *epagello*, which means "profess" or "tell, proclaim or announce".[111] He is talking here about women who are tasked with actively professing their faith, or, in other words, women who are in ministry. They should do this in an appropriate (to their faith) manner, with decency and propriety.

When Paul said that he did not want a woman to teach, was he talking about *all* women or specifically the women in Ephesus who might have been spreading heresy, for which reason he wanted them to remain silent? In any case, Paul wanted all the members of the church to behave well, so that the church would maintain a good reputation and there would be no persecution. For he had just asked the church to intercede so that they might live peaceful and quiet lives in all godliness and holiness.[112]

It is notable that Paul spoke here of "a woman" instead of women in general. There is another possibility, therefore, which is that Paul was actually talking about a specific woman whom he did not name:

> *A **woman** should learn in quietness and full submission. I do not permit **a woman** to teach or to assume authority over a man; **she** must be quiet. For Adam was formed first, then Eve. And Adam was not the one deceived; it was the woman who was deceived and became a sinner. But **women** will be saved through childbearing – if **they** continue in faith, love and holiness with propriety.[113]*

The context of Paul's instructions to Timothy is "misleading", as we can see at the beginning of the letter. There were men and women who were misleading the church by spreading false teaching. Could it be that he was talking about a specific woman who was doing this? And could it be that this one woman was therefore not allowed to teach, according to Paul, because he wanted to prevent others from being contaminated by the false teaching? Being misled is a recurring topic in Paul's letters to Timothy.[114]

Then Paul starts to speak about Eve, who was also misled, just like this woman. And he said that this woman would be saved through childbearing. Did Paul then also think that the bearing of children was the highest goal for women, just like his Greek contemporaries? Didn't Jesus clearly say that a woman would be happier if she heard and did the will of God (which also includes the command to share the gospel, which Jesus gave in Matthew)? If you were spreading heresy, then Paul was very straightforward: that had to stop immediately. Paul did not tell Timothy to send her away, but he was to correct her and teach her so that she would get back on track. That is a mercy-filled response! When Paul spoke earlier of Hymenaeus and Alexander, who were spreading blasphemous teaching, he was a lot less merciful. He even handed them over to Satan.[115]

Do you know that Jesus also forbade a misled woman to speak? It wasn't just Paul who wrote several letters; Jesus Himself had John[116] write seven letters on His behalf to seven churches. He was very upset about the misleading teaching of Balaam and the Nicolaitans.[117] Liars had entered the church. Jesus was speaking about people who claimed to be apostles but were not,[118] people who said they were Jews but were not,[119] and a woman who said she was a prophetess but was not.[120] Because of her wrong teaching some members of the church practiced harlotry and were eating food offered to idols.

People who spread misleading teaching or who were not honest should not have a voice in the church, according to the sharply worded letters of Jesus. And yet He, like Timothy, first gave this woman a chance to repent: "I have given her time to repent of her immorality, but she is unwilling."[121]

Speaking of being misled...

Eve was misled, but did you know that sin came through Adam? Some people believe that women should not teach because Eve brought sin into the world. They quote this verse: "And Adam was not the one deceived; it was the woman who was deceived and became a sinner" (1 Timothy2:14). But in his letter to the Romans Paul says: "Therefore, just as sin entered the world through one man (Adam), and death through sin, and in this way death came to all people, because all sinned."[122] The temptation came through the woman, but sin entered the world through the man. Not allowing a woman to speak because she is the guilty party is not only inconsistent, but cannot be biblically supported either.

Conclusion

We cannot know for certain whether Paul's words "I do not permit a woman to teach" prohibit a specific group of women from speaking, or just one woman who remained anonymous. It does look as if Paul is not speaking about all women. In other words: this is not a general command for all women not to teach. For if Paul did not want women to teach, why then would he work alongside so many women who did just that? In other situations, Paul does allow women to teach, as we have discovered earlier in this book: Priscilla taught Apollo, and Paul commended Phoebe.

Paul wrote a second letter to Timothy. It is remarkable that he first reminds Timothy of the faith of the women in his family. This was obviously important, and Timothy needed to hear it:

I am reminded of your sincere faith, which first lived in your grandmother Lois and in your mother Eunice and, I am persuaded, now lives in you also.[123]

Paul was convinced that Timothy shared that same faith.[124] "And the things you have heard me say in the presence of many witnesses entrust to reliable people who will also be qualified to teach others " he told him. Teaching that Timothy had learned from his mother and grandmother, and which he was now to entrust to other men and women.[125]

Timothy with his mother, who raised him in the faith. A painting by Henry Le Jeune (1870-1880).

"Yet Paul says things about women speaking in the church that even now cause a lot of confusion."

CHAPTER 9

WOMEN SHOULD REMAIN SILENT IN THE CHURCHES

Women should remain silent in the churches. They are not allowed to speak, but must be in submission, as the law says.

We have seen that Jesus empowered women to speak and that in the time of Paul women also taught and spoke. Yet Paul says something here about women speaking in the church that has been the source of many discussions and battles and even now causes a lot of confusion. What Paul said is important, because he was a significant person. Paul was an apostle called by God. He had received the best education in the traditional Jewish writings from one of the best teachers, Gamaliel.[126] He knew a lot about Jewish and Gentile cultures.

Another of his "difficult" texts is the well-known verse in 1 Corinthians 14:34: "Women should remain silent in the churches. They are not allowed to speak, but must be in submission, as the law says."

Women had to keep their mouths shut in church, according to Paul. Which churches was he speaking about? Join me as we take a look at Corinth at that time. The patroness of the city was Aphrodite, the goddess of erotic love. According to the Greek historian Strabo, the city was very popular with sailors because of all the prostitutes in the temple.

When Paul arrived in Corinth, he met the Jewish couple Aquila and Priscilla, who were tentmakers just like him. He moved in with them and they worked together at their occupation. They also preached the gospel and they started a church[127] in which people from all walks of life could be found: poor, rich, Jews, Gentiles, slaves, free men, men and of course women.[128] But the diversity was not a problem for Paul: "For we were all baptized by one Spirit so as to form one body – whether Jews or Gentiles, slave or free."[129]

Sexual immorality was also present in the church: "It is actually reported that there is sexual immorality among you, and of a kind that even pagans do not tolerate," Paul wrote in his letter to the Corinthians.[130] There was not just sexual immorality in the church; there were fights as well, as Paul was told about by the members of the house church of Chloë.

That upset him so much that he wrote a letter to the Corinthians to ask them to be united in mind and thought.[131] There was jealousy and quarreling in the churches[132] and idol worship.[133] Even during the Lord's Supper there were problems as well; some of the people were getting drunk.[134] Paul called the Corinthians immature, worldly Christians.[135] And he said that the women in these churches needed to remain silent. He added to this: "Women should remain silent in the churches. They are not allowed to speak, but must be in submission, as the law says." That last part is interesting. Because where in the law does it state that women are not allowed to speak but must be in submission? At any rate it is not listed in the 613 laws of the Old Testament. It can be found in the laws of the Jewish Talmud – the Jewish writings that are not in the Bible – and also the Greeks and Romans thought that women should not speak in public.

Paul continued: "If they want to inquire about something, they should ask their own husbands at home." Paul, like Jesus, felt that women had a right to an education and to have their questions answered. The Jews in particular excluded women from participating in religion. Paul spoke against this and encouraged women to ask questions. He wanted women to develop and he gave them a right to education. He was giving men the responsibility to help women with their education! This was a radical change from the past.

Then Paul says something quite shocking: "For it is disgraceful for a woman to speak in the church." That was indeed the case in the view of the Jews, but does Paul just agree with them, then? He did allow women to speak in other locations, didn't he? So where did this sudden statement spring from?

We know that Paul had knowledge of the Greek and Roman ideas of his day and he often quoted their poets. He was quoting Epimenides when he said: "For in him we live and move and have our being"[136] and: "One of Crete's own prophets has said it: 'Cretans are always liars, evil brutes, lazy gluttons.'"[137] He also quoted Aratus and Cleanthes: "As some of your own poets have said, 'We are his (Paul is speaking of Christ here) offspring'."[138] When he said to the Corinthians: "Do not be misled: 'Bad company corrupts good character,'" he was quoting Menander.[139] When Paul said: "For it is disgraceful for a woman to speak in the church," it could very well be that he was quoting an ancient philosopher or writer. All the more likely because nothing can be found in God's Law about a command for women to remain silent. The Old and New Testaments are full of examples of women who did speak.

In spite of the fact that we cannot find that law in the Bible, Paul did want the Corinthians to take his words seriously and obey him. We can see that as we read on. You can read it in your own Bible or here:

*Women should remain silent in the churches. They are not allowed to speak, but must be in submission, as the law says. If they want to inquire about something, they should ask their own husbands at home; for it is disgraceful for a woman to speak in the church. Or did the word of God originate with you? (In other words: are you the **prophet** here and do you know better?) Or are you the only people it has reached? (In other words: are you the **spiritually gifted person** and do you know better?) If* *anyone thinks they are a **prophet** or otherwise **gifted** by the Spirit, let them acknowledge that what I am writing to you is the Lord's command. But if anyone ignores this, they will themselves be ignored. Therefore, my brothers and sisters, be eager to prophesy, and do not forbid speaking in tongues. But everything should be done in a fitting and orderly way.*

It was obviously a serious situation if the women in Corinth needed to remain silent, because Paul emphasized his words by pointing out to the Corinthians that his writing to them is the Lord's command. Why was it a disgrace that a woman spoke? Or was *what* they were saying a disgrace? Or was Paul talking about *the way* the women were speaking and did he want to correct that? Because three chapters prior to this Paul had said that these women *were* allowed to prophesy and pray, if they did so in the correct manner:

But every woman who prays or prophesies with her head uncovered dishonors her head — it is the same as having her head shaved. For if a woman does not cover her head, she might as well have her hair cut off; but if it is a disgrace for a woman to have her hair cut off or her head shaved, then she should cover her head.[140]

Do you see the parallel with the instructions that Paul gave Timothy on how men and women were to pray (and prophesy)? In his letter to Timothy, Paul said: "Therefore I want the men everywhere to pray, lifting up holy hands without anger or disputing. I also want the women to dress modestly, with decency and propriety, adorning themselves, not with elaborate hairstyles or gold or pearls or expensive clothes, but with good deeds, appropriate for women who profess to worship God."[141]

How should men and women pray? They should not draw unnecessary attention to themselves and they should conduct themselves according to the guidelines of love: "It does not envy, it does not boast, it is not proud. It does not dishonor others, it is not self-seeking."[142]

A prophesying church

Imagine that women were not allowed to speak or preach, yet were allowed to prophesy in the church; what would that look like? Paul had envisioned that, as you can read in his letter to the Corinthians:

Follow the way of love and eagerly desire gifts of the Spirit, especially prophecy. For anyone who speaks in a tongue does not speak to people but to God. Indeed, no one understands them; they utter mysteries by the Spirit. But the one who prophesies speaks to people for their strengthening, encouraging and comfort. Anyone who speaks in a tongue edifies themselves, but the one who prophesies edifies the church. I would like every one of you to speak in tongues, but I would rather have you prophesy. The one who prophesies is greater than the one who speaks in tongues, unless someone interprets, so that the church may be edified. Now, brothers and sisters, if I come to you and speak in tongues, what good will I be to you, unless I bring you some revelation or knowledge or prophecy or word of instruction?[143]

And a little further on he said: "But if an unbeliever or an inquirer comes in while everyone is prophesying, they are convicted of sin and are brought under judgment by all."[144] Paul was super enthusiastic about prophecy here and said it was for both men and women.

Wow! That seems like a good church to me, if this is put into practice! A church in which people are edified and encouraged and when new people walk in, they are saved because people are prophesying. That sounds a lot more attractive than a church in which there are only teachers educating people. The women in Corinth needed to remain silent according to Paul, but he does encourage them to prophesy. He even mentions the prophets **before** the teachers:

And God has placed in the church first of all apostles, second prophets, third teachers, then miracles, then gifts of healing, of helping, of guidance, and of different kinds of tongues."[145]

A rose from Jesus

When I became a believer, I had a deep desire to hear God's voice. I decided to go to a conference with my friend Ineke on speaking on behalf of God. We were taught and allowed to practice understanding and giving words from God. One of the exercises was to ask God for an image, a picture for the other person. Ineke told me what she had seen for me: "I see a beautiful bouquet of flowers; they are all different. God wants to give you this bouquet, because He thinks you are precious. What do you think of that?" It reminded me immediately of my daily visits to the supermarket. I would walk past a flower shop and every day I would think: Shall I buy some flowers for myself? And then I would think: No, better not; they are too expensive. You don't buy flowers for yourself, right? I shared this with Ineke and she said: "God wants to give you these flowers, because you are worth it." I thought that was really beautiful and I held the words in my heart.

At lunch break, Ineke and I sat at a table with an older couple. We introduced ourselves and started to eat our sandwiches. At one point the man asked me: "Can I give you something?" "Of course," I said, a bit surprised. He slid a two-euro coin over the table to me and said: "Jesus wants to give you a rose. Will you promise me that you will buy a rose for yourself with this tomorrow? And then you can thank Jesus." The tears welled up inside me. How could this man have known? This had to be from God! The love of God flowed into me with those words. I was precious to Him and He showed me that with the rose. That was years ago, but as I write this and think back to those events, it still touches me deeply. I felt so special at that moment. God saw me and knew what I was thinking when I walked past that flower shop.

The next day I bought a red rose for myself at the flower shop. It stood in a vase on my dresser for months. Every time I looked at it, I had an amazing feeling in my stomach: butterflies, as if I was in love. I told everyone who would listen that I had received a rose from Jesus. Someone said to me: "I think that is very strange. You have a family, a beautiful home, a good job – everything your heart desires. And now you have a rose from Jesus, and you are like a child at Christmas." This was the beginning of a deep relationship with Jesus. Prophecy brings you closer to Him after all.[146] It can change your life. Maybe that was why Paul was so enthusiastic about the gift of prophecy.

Silent, yet prophesying

In one sentence Paul said that women should remain silent and yet he continually emphasized that there needed to be prophecy in the church – and he said it to both men and women. Why did Paul say that the women should be silent, when he also wanted them to prophesy? It seems very contradictory! Paul answered this dilemma himself:

> *What then shall we say, **brothers and sisters**? When you come together, **each of you** has a hymn, or a word of instruction, a revelation, a tongue or an interpretation. Everything must be done so that the **church** may be built up. If anyone speaks in a tongue, two – or at the most three – should speak, one at a time, and someone must interpret. If there is no interpreter, the speaker should **keep quiet** in the church and speak to himself and to God. Two or three prophets should speak, and the others should weigh carefully what is said. And if a revelation comes to someone who is sitting down, the **first speaker should stop**. For you can all prophesy in turn so that everyone may be instructed and encouraged. The spirits of prophets are subject to the control of prophets. For God is not a God of disorder but of peace – as in all the congregations of the Lord's people.[147]*

Paul seems to have had a problem with the lack of order in the church and it was not just women who were disturbing the services by talking. There seem to have been men too who did this by praying out loud in tongues, and there were people who were prophesying at the same time. Paul said that if people were praying in tongues without an interpreter, they should be silent.[148] But that does not mean that they should not pray in tongues at all; quite the opposite, as he later said: "Do not forbid speaking in tongues."[149] It should just be done in an orderly fashion: by two, or perhaps three people, each in turn, and someone should give an interpretation.[150]

Paul also said that people should not all prophesy at once.[151] If one person is prophesying, then the others should remain silent. That does not mean that Paul wanted to silence all prophets. On the contrary, he calls on the Corinthians to "eagerly desire the gifts of the Spirit, especially prophecy".[152]

Can you see that Paul was not trying to tell all women to be silent during the service? He wanted the service to be orderly. Paul encouraged everyone (men and women) to participate in the service, but it must all be to build up the church.[153] "For God is not a God of disorder but of peace – as in all the congregations of the Lord's people.[154] But everything should be done in a fitting and orderly way."[155] If everyone just does what they want, no one will be built up. And that was the whole idea. The gifts of the Spirit were meant to be used to build each other up, and the church of Corinth was lacking in that area: "You are giving thanks well enough, but no one else is edified."[156] "For you can all prophesy in turn so that everyone may be instructed and encouraged."[157]

Submission... to whom?

"Women should remain silent in the churches. They are not allowed to speak, but must be in **submission,** *as the law says." (1 Corinthians 14:34)*

In the ancient world all relationships were hierarchal, among them the relationships between a husband and wife, a father and child, and a master and slave. You can see that this was the norm for the ancient Greeks (Aristotle, Homer) and the Romans (Cicero) as well as the Jews (Berakhot, Hagigah, Shekalim). The husband was always above his wife. In Ephesians 5, where Paul spoke about the relationship between a husband and his wife, he encouraged the men and women to first *submit to each other* out of respect for God. Then he told the wives that they were to submit to their husbands: "Wives, submit yourselves to your own husbands as you do to the Lord. For the husband is the head of the wife as Christ is the head of the church, his body, of which he is the Savior. Now as the church submits to Christ, so also wives should submit to their husbands in everything."

Submission does not mean that the man is the boss of the woman. Paul drew a comparison with Christ, who is the Savior of the body. A woman can surrender herself to the protection of her husband. She can do that if he loves her as Christ loved the church:

Husbands, love your wives, just as Christ loved the church [He even gave his life!] and gave himself up for her to make her holy, cleansing her by the washing with water through the word, and to present her to himself as a radiant church, without stain or wrinkle or any other blemish, but holy and blameless. In this same way, husbands ought to love their wives as their own bodies. He who loves his wife loves himself. After all, no one ever hated their own body, but they feed and care for their body, just as Christ does the church – for we are members of his body. "For this reason, a man will leave his father and mother and be united to his wife, and the two will become one flesh." This is a profound mystery – but I am talking about Christ and the church. However, each one of you also must love his wife as he loves himself, and the wife must respect her husband. (Ephesians 5:25–33)[158]

Nowhere does Paul say that women need to obey their husbands, or, in other words, that men are the boss. He only said that to children and slaves. "Children, **obey** your parents in the Lord, for this is right. Slaves, **obey** your earthly masters with respect and fear, and with sincerity of heart, just as you would obey Christ." [159]

Greetings from Priscilla

Paul ended his first letter to the Corinthians with greetings from the church leaders Aquila and Priscilla: "The churches in the province of Asia send you greetings. Aquila and Priscilla greet you warmly in the Lord, and so does the church that meets at their house."[160] Did you know that they were actually the founders of the church? Earlier on in the letter Paul had said: "I planted the seed, Apollos watered it, but God has been making it grow."[161] Paul founded the church in Corinth with Apollos and Apollos received his education from Priscilla and Aquila, as we can read in the book of Acts:

"Meanwhile a Jew named Apollos, a native of Alexandria, came to Ephesus. He was a learned man, with a thorough knowledge of the scriptures. He had been instructed in the way of the Lord, and he spoke with great fervor and taught about Jesus accurately, though he knew only the baptism of John. He began to speak boldly in the synagogue. When Priscilla and Aquila heard him, they invited him to their home and explained to him the way of God more adequately."[162] Priscilla did not just teach members of the church; she and her husband taught one of the two *leaders* of that church.

Women and their influence on the church

There are two passages in the Bible that say women should be silent in church: in 1 Corinthians and 1 Timothy. At the same time we see that women were the ones who greatly influenced the leaders of these churches: Priscilla taught Apollos, the leader of the church in Corinth, and Lois and Eunice passed on their faith to Timothy, the leader of the church in Ephesus. These women may not have stood up on the stages of these churches, but they were of great value and meaning behind the scenes.

CHAPTER 10

BACK TO THE START

What are you thinking, now that you have read all this? When we made these discoveries, our first thoughts were: women have had a really rough time in history; we never realized how bad it was! And Jesus made such a huge difference for women.

We get all upset about whether or not a woman should wear a hat or cover her head in church, yet we read in the very same verse that women are allowed to pray and prophesy; somehow we conveniently don't notice that, though. Because for years women have had no voice in the church.

From the fall of mankind, men have ruled over women. Some Christians believe that this is God's order. If you truly believe that men should rule over women, then the Greeks, Romans and Jews did nothing wrong! Their men lorded it over their women as if they were their property.

How different God meant it to be. The desire of His heart was that men and women would rule over creation together, but not rule over each other, and that they would submit to each other. A wife should respect her husband and a husband must love his wife, because although we are of equal value we have been created differently: men mostly need respect and women mostly need love.

From the very beginning God wanted men to give up everything and to go to their wife, but what we have seen again and again in history is that it was women who had to give up everything when they were chosen by a man.

From the beginning there have been men and women who were called by God and equipped by Him with gifts to lead and teach. All of these gifts are given to build up the Body of Christ (the church). Nowhere does the Bible distinguish between men and women in this area. That makes sense, because through our faith in Jesus we are all one in Christ.[163] According to Paul, it does not matter whether you are Jew or Greek, slave or free, or whether you are a man or a woman.[164] God gives His gifts to whom He desires[165] and His choice can surprise us sometimes. When God gave the Holy Spirit to the Gentiles, the circumcised Jews in Jerusalem could not understand it. They thought that only *they* were allowed to receive the gift of the Holy Spirit. They could not prevent it, however.[166]

Throughout the ages there have been people who could not understand that women might be allowed to do the same things as men; let alone that God might have *called* them to do it. Just recently there was quite a commotion when pastor and author John MacArthur publicly belittled Bible teacher Beth Moore during a conference in California. A panel consisting of MacArthur and some other men in ministry were asked to give a spontaneous response to various things that were mentioned to them. When MacArthur was presented with the name "Beth Moore", he called out: "Go home!" When the audience had finished laughing and clapping, MacArthur explained his response: "There is no case that can be made biblically for a woman preacher. Period. End of discussion."[167]

But why would God give women gifts and then not allow them to use them? It is not God's fault that there are women who do not use their gifts and do not fulfill their calling to preach. That can occur when you, as a woman, allow yourself to be led by fear, by ruling cultural opinions or by people (leaders) who discourage you from doing this. Thankfully, throughout history we have also seen women who answered God's call and who have brought forth much fruit because of that.

The founder of The Salvation Army, General William Booth (1829–1912), once said: "Some of my best men are women!" Especially at the beginning of their evangelistic work on the streets of London, a great deal of courage was needed in order to do this work. In 1889 at least 669 members of The Salvation Army were attacked, among whom were 251 women. They were pursued and pelted with stones, mutilated and sometimes even killed. The meetings of The Salvation Army were often interrupted. Many times mud and stones were thrown at the windows. Sometimes hundreds of people stormed the meeting halls, broke windows and destroyed the interiors of buildings. Booth wrote: "The evangelists sometimes have to enter the homes in order to escape the mobs. The police refuse to protect them.

Nevertheless, many are saved. We must never give up, never!"[168] Booth had a daughter, Evangeline, who at 21 was already an officer in an area where there was a lot of resistance to The Salvation Army. When there were problems, he always said: "Send Eva!" She was the first woman to fill the position of general.

God empowers both men and women with His Spirit to be His witnesses and to fulfill the great commission, also in dangerous areas.

One of the best-known female evangelists from our country, the Netherlands, is probably Corrie ten Boom. Her parents provided shelter for Jewish refugees during the Second World War. Thanks to the secret room in their Haarlem home – which can now be visited as a museum – more than 80 Jews survived the war. But when the family was betrayed by a Nazi collaborator, Corrie and her father and sister were arrested and taken to a concentration camp. Corrie was the only one of her family who survived the camp. After the war she traveled the world to tell of God's goodness, which she had experienced during that dark period. She fulfilled her calling at the risk of losing her life and even traveled behind the Iron Curtain to Russia to share the gospel.

Billy Graham made a film of Corrie ten Boom's bestselling book "The Hiding Place".

Her testimony of how she forgave a camp executioner whom she met again after the war is world-famous. Corrie shared how she had never experienced God's love as she did at that moment. One of her best-known sayings was: "You may never know that Jesus is all you need, until Jesus is all you have."

Like no other, Billy Graham must have known the impact of a powerful woman of God on his life through the teachings of Henrietta Mears. He was committed to making Corrie ten Boom's work known worldwide and in the 1970s made a film of her bestselling book *De Schuilplaats (The Hiding Place)*. As a result, millions of people were reached with the gospel.

Imagine this: you are a woman and God has called you to fulfill a task in His Kingdom, so what do you do when people work against you or even prevent you from doing it? Mary responded in this manner to her calling: "May it be unto me as You say." In other words, what God said to her was more important. She stood firm against all of the rejection from her contemporaries and – thank God – fulfilled her calling. That could not have been easy. Can you imagine? She must have been about 14 when she became pregnant. A forbidden pregnancy, because she was not married – which carried the death penalty at the time. She had to flee multiple times because people were out to kill her child. Yet she listened to God. How did Peter and John respond when they were commanded to be silent about Jesus and were no longer allowed to teach? They said nearly the same thing as Mary: "Which is right in God's eyes: to listen to you, or to him? You be the judges! As for us, we cannot help speaking about what we have seen and heard."[169] And later they said in slightly different wording: "We must obey God rather than human beings!"[170]

We hope that this book has brought you back to the beginning. Back to where it started. Back to God's heart, which Jesus and Paul have revealed to us so beautifully. We hope that this is what you will take with you after reading this book.

God gives His gifts to men *and* women

God calls and anoints leaders, and these leaders can be both men and women. "Do not touch my anointed ones; do my prophets no harm," God says.[171] This refers to both sexes, because according to the Bible we are all wonderfully made.[172] God's gifts are spoken of at length in the Bible. The gifts of the Spirit, for example, among which are several that involve speaking: speaking in tongues, interpretation of tongues, and the gift of prophecy. These gifts are for both men and women. In the Old Testament Moses said yearningly: "I wish that all the Lord's people were prophets and that the Lord would put his Spirit on them!", instead of only on the 70 elders on whom God had poured out His Spirit.[173] His wish was fulfilled when, at Pentecost, the Spirit of God was poured out on all flesh:

"No, this is what was spoken by the prophet Joel: 'In the last days, God says, I will pour out my Spirit on all people, Your sons and daughters will prophesy, your young men will see visions, your old men will dream dreams. Even on my servants, both men and women, I will pour out my Spirit in those days, and they will prophesy.'"[174]

NOTES

1   Chronicles 7:24

2   Upper Bet Choron is now called Beit Ur al-Fawqa and Lower Bet Choron is now called Beit Ur al-Tahta (about 16 km north-west of Jerusalem). Uzzen-Seëra is identified by geographers as Beit Sira (about 4 km west of the other two places and 21 km north-west of Jerusalem).

3   Joshua 10: 10-11

4   Isaiah 53

5   Matthew 27:19

6   Matthew 27:19

7   Matthew 27:24

8   https://peoplepill.com/people/Pontius-pilates-wife/ and https://and.m.wikipedia.org/wiki/Pontius_Pilate%27s_wife

9   Exodus 1:15-20

10   Matthew 26:58, 69, 71-73; John 18:17; Mark 14:70

11   Genesis 3:15 NBG51, Galatians 4:4

12   John 2:1-12

13   Matthew 26:6-13

14   Leviticus 8:12

15   1 Samuel 16:13

16   Matthew 28:1-10

17   Acts 16:14

18   Source: Wikipedia

19   Source: historiek.net

20   For example https://www.sacred-texts.com/cla/hesiod/theogony.htm

21   Source: https://grieksemythologie.net/namen/ther/zeus.html

22   https://and.wikipedia.org/wiki/Types_of_Women: here you will find various references to the poem of Simonides in which he describes woman as animals.

23   Source: Aristotle, *The Generation of Animals*

24   This comes from the phrase "Against Neaira" which is included in the works of Demosthenes, but probably written by a contemporary.

25   "Si sine uxore pati possemus, Quirites, omnes ea molestia careremus; set quoniam ita natura tradidit, ut nec cum illis satis commode, nec sine illis ullo modo vivi possit, saluti perpetuae potius quam brevi voluptati consulendum est." (Noctes Atticae boek 1. VI)

26   https://www.historyextra.com/period/roman/ancient-rome-women-girls-facts/

27   Judges 4:4

28   2 Kings 22:14

29   1 Samuel 25:32

30   Proverbs 18:22 and 19:14

31   Luke 11:46 and Matthew 15:6

32   Mishnah Sotah 3:4

33   Mishnah Torah, Torah Study 1:13

34   Yevamot 103b

35   Nedarim 20b

36   Megilla 3:11

37   Berachot 45b

38   Deuteronomy 29:9

39   Deuteronomy 31:12

40   about 50 B.C. until 10 A.D.

41   1 Corinthians 11:4 and 5

42   1 Corinthians 11:15

43   2 Kings 22:14 and in 2 Chronicles 34:22

44   Luke 2:36

45   Isaiah 8:3

46   Acts 21:8

47   Acts 2:16

48   This was a unilateral agreement: a man may be divorced from his wife but a wife not from her husband: M. Gittin 9.10 note 25 chapter 8

49   Genesis 2:17-25

50   Exodus 18:4, Deuteronomy 33:7, Deuteronomy 33:26, Deuteronomy 33:29, Psalm 20:3, Psalm 33:20, Psalm 70:6, Psalm 89:20, Psalm 115:9-11, Psalm 121:1,2, Psalm 124:8, Psalm 146:5, Hosea 13:9

51   1 Samuel7:12

52   Genesis 2:24

53   Ephesians 6:21-33

54   Genesis 1:26

55   Genesis 1:28

56   Genesis 3:16b

57   Genesis 3:14-19

58   Genesis 3:15 NKJV

59   John 20:16

60   According to the movie *Mary Magdalene*

61   Luke 8:1-3

62   Luke 23:27-32

63   Luke 23:55

64   Luke 24: 22-23

65   Acts 1:13

66   John 6:37

67   John 8:3; Leviticus 20:10

68   John 8:6b - 11

69   Luke 13:10-17

70   Numbers 26:33 – 27:12

71   Matthew 15:21-28

72   Matthew 19:3-11

73   Mark 10:11-12

74   A collection of discussions between Jewish rabbis and learning about how you should live as a Jew

75   John 4:9

76   John 4:27a

77 Genesis 16:7-12, Genesis 21:17-19

78 Galatians 3:28

79 Mark 5:25-33

80 Leviticus 15:19-33

81 2 Peter 1:20-21

82 Acts 6:2

83 Matthew 27:55; Luke 4:38b; Luke 8:1b; Luke 10:40a

84 Luke 11:27

85 John 8:20 and John 10:23

86 Acts 22:3 "I am a Jew, born in Tarsus of Cilicia, but brought up in this city. I studied under Gamaliel and was thoroughly trained in the law of our ancestors. I was just as zealous for God as any of you are today."

87 Luke 10:39

88 John 11: 20-28

89 John 4:1-30

90 Mark 16:15

91 Luke 1:46-55

92 2 Timothy 3:16

93 From: *The Henrietta Mears Story*, Barbara Hudson Powers 1957

94 From: Mears, H. C. (1970). *431 quotes from the notes of Henrietta Mears*. E. L. Doan (Ed.). Glendale, CA: Regal Books.

95 Romans 16:3,4

96 Acts 18:2,18,26, Romans 16:3, 1 Corinthians 16:19, 2 Timothy 4:19

97 Acts 18:26b

98 Acts 18:27b

99 Acts 16:9-35

100 Philippians 4:15

101 Sometimes theologians disagree about whether someone was a woman or a man, so this number of ten is not exact.

102 Philippians 4:2

103 Romans 16:7

104 Romans 16:1-2

105 See https://www.ministrymagazine.org/archive/2013/04/phoebe-was-she-an-early-church-leader

106 1 Timothy 5:17

107 1 Timothy 2:12

108 1 Timothy 1:3

109 1 Timothy 2:1-9

110 1 Timothy 2:9-10

111 It is striking that this word G1861 is only translated twice in this letter to Timothy *as to profess* in 1 Timothy 2:10 and 1 Timothy 6:21. The other thirteen times it is always *promise*.
1 Timothy 6:20 "Timothy, guard what has been entrusted to your care. Turn away from godless chatter and the opposing ideas of what is falsely called knowledge, which some have professed (G1861) and in so doing have departed from the faith. Grace be with you all."
G1861 ep-ang-el'-lo
From G1909 and the base of G32; to announce upon (reflexively), that is, (by implication) to engage to do something, to assert something respecting oneself: - profess, (make) promise.
Total KJV occurrences: 15

112 1 Timothy 2:1-2

113 1 Timothy 2:11-15

114 2 Timothy 3:13, 1 Timothy 1:3, 1 Timothy 1:6-7

115 1 Timothy 1:19

116 Revelation 1:19

117 Revelation 2:14-15

118 Revelation 2:2

119 Revelation 2:9

120 Revelation 2:20

121 Revelation 2:21

122 Romans 5:12, 1 Corinthians 15:22, Hosea 6:6

123 2 Timothy 1:5

124 1 Timothy 4:6, 2 Timothy 1:5

125 2 Timothy 2:2

126 Acts 22:3 "I am a Jew, born in Tarsus of Cilicia, but brought up in this city. I studied under Gamaliel and was thoroughly trained in the law of our ancestors. I was just as zealous for God as any of you are today."

127 Acts 18:1-5

128   1 Corinthians 1:26b

129 1 Corinthians 12:13

130 1 Corinthians 5:1a

131 1 Corinthians 1:10, 1 Corinthians 6:1

132 1 Corinthians 3:3

133 1 Corinthians 10:14

134 1 Corinthians 11:21

135 1 Corinthians 3:2

136 Acts 17:28a

137 Titus 1:12

138 Acts 17:28b

139 1 Corinthians 15:33. The same Menander (342-191 BC) also said: "A man who teaches a woman to write is like a man who gives a snake poison."

140 1 Corinthians 11:5-6

141 1 Timothy 2:8-10

142 1 Corinthians 13:4b-5a

143 1 Corinthians 14:1-6

144 1 Corinthians 14:24

145 1 Corinthians 12:28

146 Revelation 19:10

147 1 Corinthians 14:26-33

148 1 Corinthians 14:28

149 1 Corinthians 14:39

150 1 Corinthians 14:27

151 1 Corinthians 14:29

152 1 Corinthians 14:1, 39a

153 1 Corinthians 14:26

154   1 Corinthians 14:33

155 1 Corinthians 14:40

156 1 Corinthians 14:17

157 1 Corinthians 14:31

158 A more accurate translation of the last verse (33) from the original text would mean that Paul says there that men must love their wives so that they can honor him. So, Paul did not give the women a command here. The men were the ones who had to do their best.

159 Ephesians 6:1-6

160 1 Corinthians 16:19

161 1 Corinthians 3:6

162 Acts 18:24

163 Galatians 3:28, Ephesians 4:4

164 Galatians 3:28

165 1 Corinthians 12:11

166 Acts 11:17

167 In October 2019

168 https://www.gospeltruth.net/booth/boothbioshort.htm

169 Acts 4: 18-20

170 Acts 5:29

171 1 Chronicles 16:22

172 Psalm 139:13

173 Numbers 11:26-28

174 Acts 2:16-18

JOLANDE BIJL
GIFTS FROM GOD'S GARDEN
JOLANDE BIJL
LIVING A HEALTHY AND HAPPY LIFE WITH ESSENTIAL OILS
Gifts from God's Garden

OTHER BOOKS BY JOLANDE BIJL

AVAILABLE AT AMAZON

GIFTS FROM GOD'S GARDEN

Living a healthy and happy life with essential oils

Myrrh gave queen Esther the courage to risk her life to save her people. Frankincense gave the priests clarity of spirit and thought and protected the Israelites from an epidemic. Sleeping under a juniper tree renewed the prophet Elijah's strength. What kind of amazing qualities do plants, herbs and trees possess and what can we find in the Bible about them? Is the anointing oil in the Bible the same as the essential oils used today? How Biblical is aromatherapy? In this book Jolande takes you on a journey through the Bible, in search of God's gifts in creation. Discover how you too can lead a physically, spiritually and emotionally healthy life with Biblical oils.

With an overview of 25 trees and plants in the Bible for your well-being!

UNDERSTANDING YOUR DREAMS AND VISIONS

God speaks when you are awake and when you sleep

For God speaks again and again, though people do not recognize it. He speaks in dreams, in visions of the night, when deep sleep falls on people as they lie in their beds. He whispers in their ears and terrifies them with warnings. He makes them turn from doing wrong; he keeps them from pride. (Job 33:14-17 NLT)

It is impossible to read the Bible and not notice how often God speaks to people through dreams and visions. Nevertheless, most people don't know how to interpret their dreams nor visions.

God speaks to us through dreams and visions. He does this because he desires to have an intimate relationship with us. Are you curious as to what the possible meanings of your dreams and visions could be? Do you want to know the possible messages God may be speaking to you through them? Then join me on this journey to reveal how God may be speaking to you through dreams and visions.

The Holy Spirit can help all of God's children learn how to interpret their dreams and visions. This book can be a manual to help you grow in this skill.

Activating
Your Spiritual
GIFTS
Journal
Jolande Bijl

ACTIVATING YOUR SPIRITUAL GIFTS

Practical book to both read and use as a manual, for everyone who wants to grow in the supernatural gifts of the Holy Spirit, such as: healing power, words of wisdom ad encouragement, interpretation of dreams and prophecy.

Available in both paperback and Kindle edition.